孔子学院总部/国家汉办
Confucius Institute Headquarters(Hanban)

中国的故事·地理篇
STORIES FROM CHINA

中国文化阅读丛书
A Series on Chinese Culture

Geography

刘美如（Meiru LIU）吕丽娜（Lina LU） 编著
Andrew John Bauer 翻译

PHOENIX
TREE
PUBLISHING INC.

PHOENIX TREE PUBLISHING INC.

STORIES FROM CHINA: Myths and Legends 中国的故事：地理篇
First Edition

Chinese Editor:	Yuan Jiuqiang
English Editor:	Hou Xiaojuan
Graphic Designer:	Li Jia

© 2014 PHOENIX TREE PUBLISHING INC.

ISBN: 978-1-62575-002-0

Library of Congress Control Number: 2014931228

For more information about our products, please visit www.phoenixtree.com

Photo credits: Microfotos (微图), frontfoto (前图) and CNSfoto (中国新闻图片网).

编写说明

◉ **语言教学和文化教学相结合**

通过阅读本系列读物，使学习者在培养阅读技能的同时，对中国文化有更深入的认识和了解，培养、发展学生的国际视野和跨文化交际能力。

◉ **遵循海外本土汉语阅读教材的编写特点、发展趋势**

我们的编写理念是建立在给学生"看什么"（阅读的内容）、"为什么看"（阅读原因）、"如何看"（阅读方法）的基础上的，注重教材的知识性、故事性、趣味性、实用性、适用性、可读性、易读性原则。每个故事均以启发学习者阅读兴趣的导读问题开始，增强互动性，更多地调动学生阅读前的思考，激发学生的阅读兴趣。

◉ **以国家标准和大纲为依据**

本书在编写中参考了美国国家外语协会制定的《21世纪外语学习标准》，在文中贯穿五大原则目标，即沟通（Communication）、文化（Cultures）、连贯（Connections）、比较（Comparisons）和社区（Communities），使学习者通过使用本套教材，提高运用中文进行沟通的能力，充分认识、理解和掌握中国文化，并能将其连贯到其他的专科领域，培养学习者比较不同语言文化之间特点和特性的能力，并将其运用到日常生活和学习中。

在词汇控制方面，以中国国家汉办颁布的《新汉语水平考试大纲》和《汉语国际教育用音节、汉字、词汇等级划分》为依据，对语料进行加工，控制词汇难度。

◙ 以"通过阅读学会阅读"为目的

在本系列读物的练习设计中，语言理解和课文理解两种形式的练习轻重并举、比重适量，避免过多的语法语义方面的练习，以保证阅读的趣味性，力求达到让学习者"通过阅读学会阅读"的根本目的。

适用对象

本系列读物适合具有中、高级汉语水平的学习者作为课内泛读教材或课外阅读材料。内容可根据学习者的兴趣灵活选择搭配。

主要内容

本套丛书共分十册，每册含一个文化专题，每个专题配有十个故事，每个故事约 1000 ~ 1200 个汉字，以介绍中国文化知识为目的，以提高学习者中文阅读能力为目标，内容涉及中国历史、地理、民俗、神话、文化、艺术、汉语、传统节日、文学、古今名人轶事等方方面面。

每个故事均以导读问题开始，如"中国传统武术有几种形式和派别"、"武术除了健身以外，还有什么效用"、"武术的'武'字有什么含义"等。

每篇故事配有与内容相关的图片。生词随课文同现，方便学习和阅读。练习包括阅读理解、语段练习、词汇练习、语法练习和写作练习。

主要特点

◙ 集知识性、趣味性、实用性为一体。

◙ 每课内容前后衔接而又相互独立。重复出现的生词每课都进行标注，学习者随便翻开哪一课都可以直接阅读。

◙ 课后练习与新 HSK 的测试项目相结合。

- 每个专题都自成体系，学习者可以根据自己的需要或兴趣，选择某个专题中的若干课文进行学习。
- 图文并茂，每篇文章都配有与内容相关的图片。

　　我们借此机会感谢国家汉办／孔子学院总部对本套丛书编写的大力支持，并感谢为编写本套丛书提供部分素材的老师：

　　陈苏蓉、冯凌、胡维佳、刘颖、钱景炜、吴瑶、吴莉、赵文娟。

　　也感谢协助把中文课文翻译成英文的安迪（Andrew John Bauer）。

刘美如　吕丽娜

2014 年春于美国波特兰

A Guide to the Use of This Book

Combination of language teaching with culture teaching

This series aims not only at developing students' reading skills, but also at helping them gain a deeper understanding of Chinese culture and developing their international vision and cross-cultural communication skills.

Adherence to the compilation characteristics and development trend of Chinese reading textbooks in the United Stated and in other countries

Based on the compilation ideas of helping students understand "what" to read (the contents), "why" to read (the reasons) and "how" to read (the methods), this series attaches much importance to being informative, fun, practical and easy. Each story starts with some led-in questions, which stimulate students' interest in reading, enhance interaction, and make students think before reading the story.

In accordance with the national standards and the guideline

In reference to the *Standards for Foreign Language Learning in the 21st Century* formulated by American Council on the Teaching of Foreign Languages (ACTFL), this book observes the Five Goals (Five C's), namely

Communication, Cultures, Connections, Comparisons and Communities. Upon using this series of textbooks, students will improve their communication skills in Chinese, getting thorough understanding and mastery of Chinese culture and connecting it to other disciplines. It also cultivates students' ability to compare the characteristics of different languages and cultures and apply it to their daily life and study.

In terms of vocabulary control, the series has revised its language data to control its degree of difficulty based on the *New HSK Guideline* and the *Graded Chinese Syllables, Characters and Words for the Application of Teaching Chinese to the Speakers of Other Languages* issued by Hanban of China.

The purpose of "learning reading through reading"

As for the design of exercises, this series, with equal emphasis and appropriate proportion put on the comprehension of the language and the texts, avoids too many exercises on grammar and semantics, striving to achieve the purpose of "learning reading through reading" to ensure its interestingness.

Target Readers

Targeted at learners of Chinese language at intermediate or advanced level, this series is used as an extensive reading textbook inside and outside the classroom. Students can choose what to be learned according to their interests.

Contents

There are altogether 10 volumes in the series of *Stories from China*, each with a topic about culture. Each topic is provided with 10 stories. With approximate 1000 ~ 1200 Chinese characters, each story aims at introducing information about Chinese culture and improving students' reading ability in Chinese, encompassing Chinese history, geography, folk customs, legends, culture, arts, language, traditional festivals, literature, anecdotes of celebrities in ancient and contemporary times, and other aspects.

Each story starts with some led-in questions, such as "What forms and schools do the traditional Chinese martial arts have?", "Besides keeping fit, what can martial arts be used for?", and "What's the meaning of '武' in '武术' (martial arts)?"

Pertinent illustrations are provided for each story. Concurrently presented with the text, new words are placed on the right side of the text to facilitate students' learning and reading. Exercises are composed of the following parts: Reading comprehension, Exercises about paragraphs, Exercises about vocabulary, Exercises about grammar, Writing practice, and so on.

Features

- Integrating informativeness with interestingness and practicalness
- Each text is both connected with each other and independent from each other. With the new words repeatedly marked and explained in each lesson, students can understand them in any lesson they read.
- Exercises after each lesson are integrated to the questions in the new HSK test.

- Each topic is independent from each other. Therefore, students are free to choose a text under a certain topic based on their need or interest.
- Each story is provided with beautiful content-based illustrations.

Acknowledgements

We would like to take this opportunity to thank Hanban/the Confucius Institute Headquarters for its support in the writing of this book series, and those who helped with some initial information collecting and sorting. They are: Chen Surong, Feng Ling, Hu Weijia, Liu Ying, Qian Jingwei, Wu Yao, Wu Li, and Zhao Wenjuan.

We would also like to thank Andrew John Bauer for his help with the translation of the texts into English.

Liu Meiru & Lu Lina

Spring 2014 in Portland of the United States of America

目录

中国的位置和行政区划

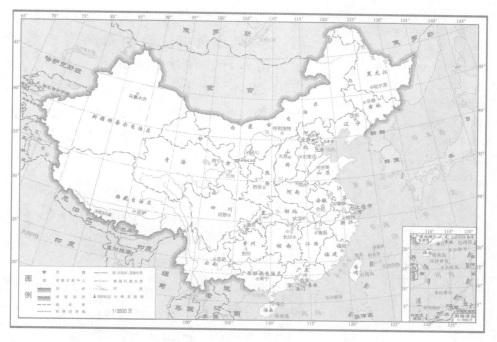

中国行政区划图

导读问题　Lead-in questions

1. 请在上面的地图中找出中国的首都。
2. 中国的地理位置（location）在哪儿？中国的邻居（neighbor）都有哪些国家？
3. 世界上陆地面积排名前三位的国家是哪三个？它们分别在哪个洲？
4. 你知道中国有哪些省、直辖市、自治区和特区吗？
5. 中国面积最大的省是哪个？人口最多的省是哪个？

亚欧　Yà-Ōu
Asia and Europe

大陆　dàlù
continent, mainland

边界　biānjiè
border, boundary

邻居　línjū
neighbor

海洋　hǎiyáng
sea, ocean

相连　xiānglián
to connect

排名　pái míng
to rank

跨越　kuàyuè
to span

中国位于亚欧大陆东部，太平洋西岸，陆地上的边界长达2万多公里。中国的东边有朝鲜，北边是俄罗斯和蒙古，西北有哈萨克斯坦、吉尔吉斯斯坦、塔吉克斯坦，西和西南有巴基斯坦、阿富汗、印度、尼泊尔、不丹，南边与缅甸、老挝、越南相接，共有14个邻居。中国的东边和南边有渤海、黄海、东海和南海，跟世界上最大的海洋——太平洋相连。

位于中国南海边上的三亚风光

中国的陆地面积约960万平方公里，在世界上排第三位。排名第一的是俄罗斯，第二是加拿大，美国排名第四。从中国最南端到最北端、从最东端到最西端，全长都有5000多公里。中国东西跨越5个时区，当住在东部的学生早上背着书包去上学的时候，住在西部的小

China is located in eastern Eurasia on the western shores of the Pacific Ocean with the national border totaling more than 20000 kilometers. To the east, China is bounded by Korea, to the north by Russia and Mongolia, to the northwest by Kazakhstan, Kyrgyzstan, Tajikistan, to the west and

黄海、渤海交界处的山东烟台万鸟岛

southwest by Pakistan, Afghanistan, India, Nepal and Bhutan, etc, and to the south by Myanmar, Laos and Vietnam, with 14 neighbors in total. There are Bohai Sea, Yellow Sea, the East Sea, and the South Sea to the east and south of China, which are connected with the world's largest ocean, the Pacific Ocean.

China has a total land area of 9.6 million square kilometers, ranking it the third in the world. Russia ranks the first in land area and Canada follows. The United States is the fourth largest country. From China's southernmost part to its northernmost, and from its easternmost part to its

背着书包去上学的南方孩子

岛屿　dǎoyǔ
island

民族　mínzú
ethnic group, nationality

因素　yīnsù
factor

区域　qūyù
area

直辖市　zhíxiáshì
municipality directly under
the Central Govemment

地位　dìwèi
status

坐落　zuòluò
to be situated

首都　shǒudū
capital of a country

朋友们还在呼呼地睡大觉呢。除了陆地面积以外，中国还有约 473 万平方公里的海洋面积，有 5000 多个岛屿，其中，台湾岛是中国最大的岛屿。

台湾著名景点日月潭风光

中国人口目前已经超过 13 亿。这么大的一个国家怎么管理呢？中国政府根据政治、经济、民族、历史、地理等各种不同的因素，把全国划分为大小不同的区域。现在中国一共有 23 个省、5 个民族自治区、4 个直辖市、2 个特别行政区，加起来一共是 34 个行政区。

直辖市是在政治、经济、文化等方面具有特别重要地位的大城市。这 4 个直辖市是北京市、天津市、上海市和重庆市。北京市坐落在华北平原北部，是中国的首都，也是中国的政治、文化、科学和教育中心，以及重要交通枢

westernmost, the lengths both total more than 5000 kilometers. The areas from the east to the west in China span 5 time zones. When the pupils in the eastern regions of China are heading for their schools with their schoolbags on their backs, the kids in western China are still in a sound sleep. Other than land area, China also possesses about 4.73 million square kilometers of sea area, with more than 5000 islands, among which the Island of Taiwan is China's largest island.

Currently, the population of China has already exceeded 1.3 billion. So how is such a large country administered? The Chinese government has divided the country into a number of administrative regions based on political, economic, ethnical, historic, geographic and various other factors. In China, there are currently 23 provinces, 5 ethnic autonomous regions, 4 municipalities directly under the Central Govemment, and 2 special administrative regions, totaling 34 administrative regions.

Municipalities directly under the Central Govemment are large cities of particularly important status in regard of politics, economy, and culture, etc.

上海陆家嘴风光

港口　gǎngkǒu
port

乘　chéng
to take (a bus, train, etc.)

城际　chéngjì
inter-city

高铁　gāotiě
high-speed rail

单程　dānchéng
one-way

沿海　yánhǎi
coastal

举足轻重　jǔzú qīngzhòng
to play a decisive role

上游　shàngyóu
upstream

枢纽　shūniǔ
hub

纽。天津市是中国北部的主要的工商业城市，同时也是中国北部最大的港口城市，是中国远洋运输、近海运输和对外贸易的重要港口。天津离北京大约 120 公里，乘京津城际高铁①单程只需要半个小时左右。上海市位于中国的东部沿海，中国最长的河流长江由西向东经上海流入大海；作为中国重要的工业基地和海港，上海在全国经济中具有举足轻重的地位。重庆市是中国西南地区最大的工商业中心，也是长江上游水陆交通枢纽。

天津海河两岸风光

中国的 2 个特别行政区是香港和澳门。

民族自治区是中国少数民族聚居的地方，由少数民族自己管理本民族内部事务。1949 年中华人民共和国成立后，

The four municipalities are Beijing, Tianjin, Shanghai and Chongqing. Situated in the northern part of the Northern China Plain, Beijing is the capital of China, as well as the political, economic, scientific and cultural center of China and an important traffic hub. Tianjin is a major industrial and commercial city in north China, and it is also

重庆朝天门码头

the largest port city in north China. It is about 120 kilometers away from Beijing, and a one-way trip by the inter-city high-speed rail only takes about 30 minutes from Tianjin to Beijing. It is an important port in China's long and short distance ocean shipping as well as foreign trade. Shanghai is located in east China along the sea. Yangtze River, the longest river in China, flows from the west to the east, passes through Shanghai and pours into the sea. As an important industrial base and seaport, Shanghai plays a

decisive role in national economy. Being the biggest industrial and commercial center in southwest China, Chongqing is also the hub land and water transportation of the upstream of Yangtze River.

The two special administrative regions of China are Hong Kong and Macau.

香港维多利亚港风光

共建立了5个民族自治区：内蒙古自治区、新疆维吾尔自治区、广西壮族自治区、宁夏回族自治区和西藏自治区。

澳门风光

中国的23个省分布在中国的内地和东部沿海地区。其中，青海省和四川省的面积最大，河南省和山东省人口最多。

中国幅员辽阔，人口众多，56个民族组成了中华民族的和谐大家庭。

新疆维吾尔族的人们能歌善舞

分布　fēnbù
to distribute

内地　nèidì
inland

组成　zǔchéng
to consist of, to compose

和谐　héxié
harmony

The ethnic autonomous regions are where the China's minority ethnic groups live and manage their own affairs. In 1949, after the People's Republic of China was founded, 5 ethnic autonomous regions were established: the Inner Mongolia Autonomous Region, Xinjiang Uygur Autonomous Region, Guangxi Zhuang Autonomous Region, Ningxia Hui Autonomous Region and Tibet Autonomous Region.

China's 23 provinces are distributed in China's inland as well as the eastern coastal areas. Among them, Qinghai Province and Sichuan Province have the largest land areas and Henan Province and Shandong Province boast the largest populations.

China has a vast territory and large population, whose 56 ethnic groups compose a large harmonious family.

位于广西大新县的德天瀑布

文化注释

❶ 城际高铁

　　铁路的一种，是指在距离比较近的两个城市之间的快速铁路，特点是相对短距离、公交化、速度快，非常方便。近年来，中国铁路发展很快，开通了很多城际列车，例如，从北京坐京津城际高铁到天津，全程只需半个小时左右，最高时速近 350 公里。城际高铁的开通，为人们的出行提供了很多方便。

◇ 练习 ◇

■ 阅读理解 Reading comprehension

练习 1：判断正误 Decide whether the following statements are right（√）or wrong（×）

例 中国位于亚欧大陆西部，太平洋东岸。（ × ）

1. 俄罗斯和蒙古在中国的西南边。（　　）

2. 中国的西南和南边有哈萨克斯坦、吉尔吉斯斯坦和塔吉克斯坦。（　　）

3. 中国的西边不邻海。（　　）

4. 中国的陆地面积比美国小，但是比俄罗斯大。（　　）

5. 台湾岛是全世界最大的岛屿。（　　）

6. 中国政府把全国划分为大小不同的区域。（　　）

7. 现在中国一共有 23 个省、5 个民族自治区、6 个直辖市、3 个特别行政区。（　　）

8. 中国一共有 36 个行政区。（　　）

9. 4 个直辖市是北京市、天津市、上海市和广州市。（　　）

10. 天津市是中国西部的主要工商业城市，同时也是西部最大的港口城市。
　　（　　）

练习2：选择正确答案 **Choose the right answers**

例 中国 ___B___ 亚欧大陆东部，太平洋西岸。

    A. 坐落   B. 位于   C. 划分   D. 邻海

1. 北京市坐落在 _____ ，是中国的首都。

    A. 华北平原北部   B. 东部沿海

    C. 中国西南地区   D. 长江上游

2. _____ 不是中国的直辖市。

    A. 天津市   B. 上海市   C. 重庆市   D. 成都市

3. 民族自治区是中国 _____ 的地方，由少数民族自己管理本民族内部事务。

    A. 人口比较集中   B. 具有特别重要地位

    C. 工商业中心   D. 少数民族聚居

4. _____ 在中国的南边。

    A. 越南   B. 阿富汗   C. 蒙古   D. 俄罗斯

5. 中国的 _____ 有渤海、黄海、东海和南海。

    A. 西边和南边   B. 东边和北边

    C. 东边和西边   D. 东边和南边

6. 中国陆地面积在世界上排名 _____ 。

    A. 第一   B. 第二   C. 第三   D. 第四

7. 乘京津城际高铁从北京到天津单程需要大约 _____ 。

    A. 一个小时   B. 一个半小时   C. 半个小时   D. 半天

8. 中国最长的河流经由_____入海。

    A. 北京   B. 天津   C. 上海   D. 南京

9. 中国人口最多的省是_____。

    A. 江苏省和浙江省   B. 广东省和海南省

    C. 青海省和四川省   D. 河南省和山东省

10. 中国幅员辽阔，人口众多，有_____个民族。

    A. 65   B. 56   C. 50   D. 60

二 语段练习 Exercises about paragraphs

连线 Match the statements on the left with those on the right

1. 中国陆地上的边界长达   A. 第三位

2. 重庆市是中国西南地区   B. 香港和澳门

3. 中国的 2 个特别行政区是   C. 太平洋

4. 中国面积最大的省是   D. 2 万多公里

5. 中国的陆地面积在世界上排名   E. 473 万平方公里

6. 直辖市是在政治、经济、文化   F. 跟世界上最大的大洋太平洋相连
   等方面

7. 与中国相邻的最大海洋是   G. 最大的工商业中心

8. 中国的西和西南有   H. 具有特别重要地位的大城市

9. 渤海、黄海、东海和南海   I. 巴基斯坦、阿富汗、印度等国家

10. 中国的海洋面积大约有   J. 青海省和四川省

三 词汇练习 Exercises about vocabulary

用本课所学的新词填空 Fill in the blanks with the words in this lesson

位于	邻居	睡大觉	跨越	港口
划分	海港	排名	东部	管理

　　中国位于亚欧大陆东部，和 14 个国家是陆上 <u>邻居</u>。中国的陆地面积目前在世界上_____是第三位。从中国最东端到最西端全长约 5000 多公里，_____5 个时区。也就是说，当那些住在_____的人们早上起床的时候，住在西部的人们还在_____呢。为了_____这么大的一个国家，中国政府把全国_____成 23 个省、5 个民族自治区、4 个直辖市和 2 个特别行政区，加起来一共是 34 个行政区。4 个直辖市是北京市、天津市、上海市和重庆市。北京市是中国的政治、文化、科学和教育中心，以及重要交通枢纽。上海市是中国重要的工业基地和_____。天津市是中国北部的主要工商业城市，同时也是中国北部最大的_____城市。_____长江上游的重庆市，是中国西南地区最大的工商业中心。中国的 2 个特别行政区是香港和澳门。

四 语法练习 Exercises about grammar

用所给的词语组句 *Make sentences with the words given*

例　亚欧大陆　太平洋　中国　东部　位于　西岸

　　<u>中国位于亚欧大陆东部，太平洋西岸。</u>

1. 排　在世界上　陆地面积　第三位　中国的

_____

2. 全长　最南端　中国　5000多公里　最北端　从……到

_____

3. 还有　除了　以外　中国　海洋面积　约473万平方公里的　陆地面积

_____

4. 区域　划分为　把　大小不同的　全国　中国政府

_____

5. 举足轻重的　上海　地位　全国经济　具有　在　中

_____

五 写作练习 Writing practice

用下列词语造句 Make sentences using the following words and phrases

1. A 跟 B 相连：_____

2. 从……到……：_____

3. 当……的时候：_____

4. 除了……以外，还有……：_____

5. 根据……把……划分为……：_____

6. 坐落在：_____

7. 交通枢纽：_____

8. 由……向……

9. 举足轻重：_____

10. 幅员辽阔：_____

地形和地势

2

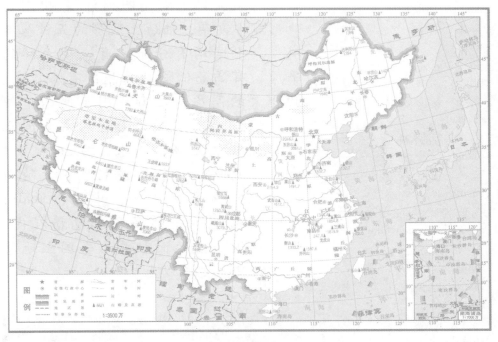

中国地形分布图

导读问题　Lead-in questions

1. 根据上图，你能看出中国哪种地形的比重最大吗？
2. 中国的地势和地形有什么特点？
3. 为什么中国的耕地资源不足？
4. 什么是中国地势的三大阶梯？中国的高原、平原和盆地是怎样围绕着三大阶梯分布的？
5. 为什么中国的大城市和人口都集中在东部？

地形 dìxíng landform	
陆地 lùdì land	
形态 xíngtài form	
丘陵 qiūlíng hill	
高原 gāoyuán plateau	
平原 píngyuán plain	
盆地 péndì basin	
高低起伏 gāo dī qǐfú ups and downs, rolling	
趋势 qūshì trend	
类型 lèixíng type	
海拔 hǎibá altitude	
崎岖 qíqū rugged	
多种多样 duōzhǒng duōyàng various	

地形是陆地表面的五种形态：山地、丘陵、高原、平原和盆地。地势指的是陆地表面高低起伏的趋势，如亚洲的地势就是"中间高四周低"。中国的地形非常复杂，陆地上地形的五种基本类型，中国均有分布。有一望无际的平原，有高高低低的丘陵，有海拔高、面积大的高原，还有周围是高山中间很低的盆地。中国的山地约占全国土地总面积的 33％，高原占约 26％，盆地约占 19％，平原约占 12％，丘陵约占 10%。如果把高山、中山、低山、丘陵和崎岖不平的高原都包括在内，那么中国山区的面积要占全国土地总面积的三分之二以上。

新疆伊犁风光

中国多种多样的地形为发展农业、

16

Landform refers to five forms of terrestrial surface: mountainous areas, hills, plateaus, plains and basins. Topography refers to the trend of ups and downs of the land surface, for example, the topography of Asia is "high in the

云南罗平丘陵地区

middle surrounded by low lands". China's landform is very complicated, with distribution of all the 5 basic types on its land. It has plains expanding as far as the eye can see, rolling hills, large plateaus high above sea level, and very low basins with high mountains around them. China's mountainous areas occupy about 33% of the total land area, followed by 26% of plateaus, 19% of basins, 12% of plains and 10% of hilly lands. If you were to include the high mountains, mid-sized mountains and low mountains, the hills and the rugged plateaus, then the mountainous area of China would account for more than two-thirds of the total land area.

The variety of landforms of China has proved to be beneficial for the development of agriculture, forestry, animal husbandry, and sideline production among others. Mountainous areas are advantageous for the

畜牧业　xùmùyè
animal husbandry

副业　fùyè
sideline production

耕地　gēngdì
arable land

地势　dìshì
terrain

阶梯　jiētī
ladder

边缘　biānyuán
edge, marginal

一系列　yíxìliè
a series of

宽广　kuānguǎng
wide

广阔　guǎngkuò
broad

包括　bāokuò
to include

林业、畜牧业和副业等多种经营提供了有利条件。山区在发展林业、牧业、旅游业和采矿业等方面具有优势，但是山区地面崎岖，交通不便，不利于发展种植业。中国山区面积广大，平原面积小，所以中国的耕地资源不足。

内蒙古呼伦贝尔草原上的羊群

　　中国地势的特点是西高东低，呈三级阶梯状分布：第一级阶梯——中国西南部的青藏高原，平均海拔在4000米以上，被称作"世界屋脊"。第二级阶梯在青藏高原边缘以东和以北，是一系列宽广的高原和巨大的盆地，海拔下降到1000～2000米。第三级阶梯在中国东部，主要是丘陵和平原，大部分地区海拔在500～1000米。第三级阶梯往东即第四阶梯，是近海的大陆架和浅海区。中国的大陆架比较广阔，包括渤海

development of forestry, livestock, tourism and mining, while the rugged land surface inconvenient for transportation is disadvantageous for the development of plantation in mountainous areas. China's mountainous areas are large, but plain areas are small, therefore, China's arable land resources are insufficient.

China's terrain characteristic can be described as high in the west and low in the east, with a three-step-ladder distribution. The first step is the Qinghai-Tibet Plateau in China's southwest, with an average elevation of over 4000 meters. It is also referred to as the "Roof of the World". The second step is the areas to the east and the north of the Qinghai-Tibet Plateau. It is a series of high plateaus and large basins, with elevations between 1000 and 2000 meters. The third step is the eastern area of China, which are mainly comprised of hills and plains, most of which are between

青藏高原阿里地区

19

平坦　píngtǎn
flat

一望无际　yíwàng wújì
endless

行使　xíngshǐ
to exercise

覆盖　fùgài
to cover

石灰岩　shíhuīyán
limestone

流水　liúshuǐ
flowing water

溶解　róngjiě
to dissolve

侵蚀　qīnshí
erosion; to erode

石芽　shíyá
clint

奇异　qíyì
bizarre

喀斯特　kāsītè
karst

和黄海的全部，东海的大部，以及南海的一部分。

　　青藏高原、内蒙古高原、黄土高原和云贵高原这四大高原，集中分布在地势的第一、二级阶梯上。青藏高原平均海拔在 4000 米以上，是世界上海拔最高的高原。内蒙古高原海拔一般在 1000 米左右，地面比较平坦，很多地方是一望无际的原野，有些地方，汽车可以自由地行驶。黄土高原因地面覆盖着厚厚的黄土而得名，这里是世界上面积最大的黄土分布区。云贵高原上石灰岩分布广泛，石灰岩被流水不断地溶解侵蚀，形成石芽、石林、峰林、溶洞等奇异的喀斯特地形。

著名的九寨沟位于四川的高山中

中国有塔里木盆地、准噶尔盆地、

云贵高原上的玉龙雪山

500-1000 meters in elevation. The third step moves towards the east to the fourth, which is the continental shelf along the sea and the shallow sea areas. China's continental shelf is wide, including the entire Bohai Sea and Yellow Sea, the majority of the East Sea as well as part of the South Sea.

Qinghai-Tibet Plateau, the Inner Mongolia Plateau, the Loess Plateau, and Yunnan-Guizhou Plateau are the four large plateaus distributed in the first and second steps of the ladder. Qinghai-Tibet Plateau, being on an average of over 4000 meters above sea level, is the highest plateau in the world. The Inner Mongolia Plateau, at an elevation of approximately 1000 meters with rather flat land, has endless open country in many areas, and there are some areas that vehicles can run effortlessly. The Loess Plateau derives its name from the thick loess covering it, and it is the area with the largest coverage of loess in the world. Limestone distribution on Yunnan-

塔里木盆地　Tǎlǐmù Péndì
Tarim Basin

塔克拉玛干沙漠
Tǎkèlāmǎgān Shāmò
Taklamakan desert

吐鲁番　Tǔlǔfān
Turpan

土壤　tǔrǎng
soil

肥沃　féiwò
fertile

汾渭平原　Fén Wèi Píngyuán
Fenwei Plain

柴达木盆地和四川盆地四大盆地，除了柴达木盆地以外，其他都分布在第二级阶梯上。塔里木盆地是中国最大的盆地，盆地中央的塔克拉玛干沙漠是中国最大的沙漠，也是世界上最大的流动沙漠。另外著名的吐鲁番盆地也分布在地势第二级阶梯上，它是中国地势最低的盆地（−155米）。

吐鲁番盆地内的葡萄沟盛产葡萄

中国的东北平原、华北平原和长江中下游平原这三大平原，分布在中国东部的第三级阶梯上。这三大平原南北相连，土壤肥沃，是中国最重要的农耕区。除此以外，中国还有成都平原、汾渭平原、珠江三角洲和台湾西部平原等，它们也都是重要的农耕区。

西高东低的地势，也对中国的生产、

Guizhou Plateau is extensive. Here limestone has been constantly dissolved and eroded by running water, thus taking shape to clints, stone forests, peak forests, limestone caves, and other bizarre karst landforms.

China has four large basins: Tarim Basin, Jungar Basin, Tsaidam

塔克拉玛干沙漠

Basin and Sichuan Basin. Other than Tsaidam Basin, all the rest are situated on the second step of the ladder. Tarim Basin is the largest basin in China, and Taklamakan Desert in the center of Tarim Basin is China's largest desert, as well as the world's largest flowing desert. Furthermore, the famous Turpan Basin is also distributed on the second step of the ladder and it is the lowest basin in China (around −155 meters in elevation).

The Northeast Plain, the North China Plain and the Middle-Lower Yangtze Plain are distributed in east China on the third step of the ladder. These three large plains are connected from north to south and covered with fertile soil. They are China's most important agricultural area. Other than these, China also has Chengdu Plain, Fenwei Plain,

华北平原风光

黄河上的李家峡水电站

沟通 gōutōng
to link up; communication

落差 luòchā
drop

蕴藏 yùncáng
reserve

湿润 shīrùn
moist

生活产生了很大的影响。第一，这样的地势，使得大部分河流都向东流，为东部地区带来了丰富的水资源，促进了东部广大地区的农业发展；第二，河流沟通了东西之间的交通，方便了沿海和内陆的经济联系，有利于促进沿海地区的经济发展和西部地区的经济大开发；第三，地势西高东低，造成河流落差大，所以河流蕴藏的水能丰富，因此在各大河流上都建有很多水力发电站①；第四，这样的地势有利于海洋上湿润气流深入内陆，带来降水；第五，西部主要是高原和大山，东部大多是平原地区，所以中国主要的大城市几乎都集中在东部，比如北京、天津、上海和广州等。

Zhujiang Delta, and Taiwan Western Plain among others. They are also important agricultural areas.

The terrain of China, which is high in the west and low in the east, has made a significant impact on the production and life in China. Firstly, such terrain makes most rivers flow eastward, bringing abundant water resources to eastern areas; therefore, it has promoted the agricultural development in the eastern areas. Secondly, the rivers link up transportation between the east and the west, making the economic connections between the coastal and inland areas convenient and have promoted the economic development of the coastal areas and the western regions. Thirdly, the terrain being high in the west and low in the east has brought about large drops in rivers; therefore, reserves of hydro-energy are rich, and many hydro-power generation stations have been constructed along big rivers. Fourthly, such terrain is beneficial in allowing the moist air current above the sea to flow inland and thus to bring precipitation. Fifthly, in the western regions, there are predominantly plateaus and high mountains and in the east mostly plain areas; therefore, almost all the major Chinese cities are found in eastern China, for example, Beijing, Tianjin, Shanghai and Guangzhou among others.

广州奥林匹克体育中心

文化注释

❶ 长江上的水电站

　　长江上有大大小小很多水电站，水能利用率达 20%。最大的是三峡水电站，最早的是葛洲坝水电站。

◇ 练习 ◇

阅读理解 Reading Comprehension

练习1：判断正误 Decide whether the following statements are right（ √ ）or wrong（ × ）

例　地形是陆地表面的五种形态：山地、丘陵、高原、平原和海洋。（ × ）

1. 地势指的是陆地表面高低起伏的趋势。（　　）

2. 亚洲的地势就是"中间低四周高"。（　　）

3. 中国高原的面积占全国土地总面积的三分之二以上。（　　）

4. 中国的耕地资源不足是因为平原较少。（　　）

5. 中国地势的特点是西低东高。（　　）

6. 中国西南部的青藏高原被称作"世界屋脊"。（　　）

7. 中国的丘陵和平原主要分布在中国东部。（　　）

8. 四大高原集中分布在第二级阶梯上。（　　）

9. 准噶尔盆地、柴达木盆地分布在第一级阶梯上。（　　）

10. 塔克拉玛干沙漠是世界上最大的流动沙漠。（　　）

练习2：选择正确答案 Choose the right answers

例 中国山区的面积 ___B___ 全国土地总面积的三分之二以上。

    A. 有   B. 占   C. 在   D. 是

1. 中国有 _____ 的平原，有高高低低的丘陵，有海拔高的高原，还有中间低、周围高的盆地。

    A. 一望无际   B. 地面崎岖   C. 资源不足   D. 第一级阶梯

2. 中国的四大高原包括：青藏高原、内蒙古高原、黄土高原和 _____。

    A. 东北高原   B. 华北高原   C. 云贵高原   D. 长江高原

3. 中国的四大盆地包括：塔里木盆地、准噶尔盆地、柴达木盆地和 _____。

    A. 吐鲁番盆地   B. 塔克拉玛干盆地

    C. 云贵盆地   D. 四川盆地

4. 世界上最大的流动沙漠在 _____ 中央。

    A. 塔里木盆地   B. 准噶尔盆地   C. 柴达木盆   D. 四川盆地

5. 中国的三大平原，分布在中国东部的 _____ 上。

    A. 第三级阶梯   B. 第二级阶梯   C. 第一级阶梯   D. 世界屋脊

6. 三大平原南北相连，土壤肥沃，是中国最重要的 _____。

    A. 黄土区   B. 林区   C. 山区   D. 农耕区

7. 黄土高原是世界上面积最大的 _____。

    A. 石灰岩分布区   B. 黄土分布区   C. 水域区   D. 农业种植区

8. 中国西南部的青藏高原，平均海拔在 _____。

    A. 4000 米以上   B. 1000 ～ 2000 米

    C. 4000 米以下   D. 400 米以下

9. 地势西高东低，造成河流 _____ ，所以在各大河流上都建有很多水力发电站。

    A. 覆盖着厚厚的黄土   B. 中间高四周低

    C. 占全国土地总面积的三分之二   D. 落差大

10. 中国主要的大城市几乎都集中在 _____ 。

    A. 高原   B. 西部   C. 东部   D. 盆地

语段练习 Exercises about paragraphs

连线 **Match the statements on the left with those on the right**

1. 中国地势的特点是	A. 山区面积广大，平原较少
2. 中国的山地约占	B. 青藏高原以东和以北
3. 山区有利于发展	C. 东部的第三级阶梯上
4. 中国的耕地资源不足是因为	D. 西高东低
5. 青藏高原位于中国的	E. 中国地势最低的盆地
6. 第二级阶梯分布在	F. 产生了很大的影响
7. 吐鲁番盆地是	G. 几乎都集中在东部
8. 中国的三大平原都分布在	H. 全国土地总面积的 33%
9. 西高东低的地势对中国的生产	I. 西南部
10. 中国主要的大城市	J. 林业、牧业、旅游业和采矿业等

词汇练习 Exercises about vocabulary

用本课所学的新词填空 **Fill in the blanks with the words in this lesson**

分布	平原	宽广	地势	丰富
沟通	影响	沙漠	世界屋脊	促进

中国 __地势__ 的特点是西高东低，分三级阶梯：中国西南部的青藏高原是第一级阶梯，被称作"_____"。青藏高原边缘以东和以北有_____的高原和巨大的盆地，这是第二级阶梯。第三级阶梯是指中国东部的丘陵和_____。中国有四大高原，它们是青藏高原、内蒙古高原、黄土高原和云贵高原，集中_____在地势第一、二级阶梯上。中国的四大盆地是塔里木盆地、准噶尔盆地、柴达木盆地和四川盆地。塔里木盆地是中国最大的盆地，盆地中央的塔克拉玛干沙漠是中国最大的_____，也是世界上最大的流动沙漠。中国的东北平原、华北平原和长江中下游平原这三大平原，分布在中国东部的第三级阶梯上。西高东低的地势，也对中国的生产、生活产生了很大的_____，例如，大部分河流都向东流，为东部地区带来了_____的水资源，_____了东部广大地区的农业发展；而且，这些河流_____了东西之间的交通，方便了沿海和内陆的经济联系，在各大河流上都建有很多水力发电站。

四 语法练习 Exercises about grammar

用所给的词语组句 Make sentences with the words given

例 青藏高原 "世界屋脊" 被称作 西南部的 中国

中国西南部的青藏高原被称作"世界屋脊"。

1. 发展 提供了 多种多样的 为 地形 有利条件 农业、林业和牧业等

_____

2. 由于 所以 耕地 山区 中国的 广大 资源不足 面积

_____

3. 全国　三分之二　中国山区的　占　面积　以上　土地总面积的

_____

4. 流动沙漠　塔克拉玛干沙漠是　中央的　在塔里木盆地　最大的　世界上

_____

5. 影响　地势　中国的　对　产生了　生产和生活　很大的　西高东低的

_____

五 写作练习 Writing practice

用下列词语造句 **Make sentences using the following words and phrases**

1. 有……有……还有……：_____

2. 一望无际：_____

3. 如果……那么……：_____

4. 为……提供了……：_____

5. 在……方面具有优势：_____

6. 因……而得名：_____

7. 除此以外：_____

8. 对……产生……影响：_____

9. 为……带来……：_____

10. 有利于：_____

人口与民族 ③

2009 年国庆时北京天安门广场的方阵

导读问题 Lead-in questions

1. 世界上人口最多的国家是哪个？
2. 中国为什么在 20 世纪 70 年代末实行了计划生育（family planning）政策？
3. 中国人口分布（distribution）的特点是什么？为什么有这样的特点？
4. 为什么说中国的 56 个民族（nationality, ethnic group）是一个大家庭？
5. 中国城镇（cities and towns）和乡村人口和经济发展有什么差别？为什么？

截止　jiézhǐ
by (a specified time), as of

赤道　chìdào
equator

圈　quān
circle

计划生育　jìhuà shēngyù
family planning

政策　zhèngcè
policy

提倡　tíchàng
to advocate

夫妇　fūfù
couple, husband and wife

控制　kòngzhì
to control

贡献　gòngxiàn
contribution

中国是世界上人口最多的国家。截止到 2010 年 11 月 1 日，中国人口总数达到 13.7 亿，大概占世界总人口的 22%，也就是说，世界上每 5 个人中就有 1 个中国人。有人曾经计算过，如果这 13.7 亿人手拉手排成 1 条线，可以绕地球赤道 26 圈。

上海七宝老街上拥挤的人群

虽然人力资源是宝贵的，但是过多的人口不但会影响经济的发展，而且对居住环境也没有好处，因此，早在 20 世纪 70 年代末，中国政府就开始实行了计划生育政策，提倡一对夫妇只生一个孩子。30 多年来，计划生育政策有效地控制了人口的迅速增长，为中国的经济发展和人民生活水平的提高做出了很大的贡献。不过，目前计划生育政策也在调整。

China is the most populous country in the world. As of November 1st, 2010, the total population of China has reached 1.37 billion, accounting for approximately 22% of the world's population, which means that one in every five

春节期间的火车站售票处，人山人海

people in the world are Chinese. Someone once made a calculation: if all these 1.37 billion people were to stand in a line hand in hand, the line would circle the equator 26 times.

Although human resources are precious, excessive population can not only affect economic development, but also do harm to the living environment. Therefore, the Chinese government has been implementing the family planning policy since the end of 1970s, advocating one child per couple. For over 30 years, the family planning policy has effectively

controlled the rapid growth of the population, and it has made a great contribution to the economic development of China and the improvement of people's living standard. However, currently the family planning policy in the midst of adjustment.

一般的家庭一对夫妻只生一个孩子

分布　fēnbù
distribution

均衡　jūnhéng
balanced

中国的人口分布很不均衡，总的特点是：东多西少。东部沿海一带的人口多于西部的人口。94% 的中国人口居住在占全国土地面积 42.9% 的东南部地区，大概只有 6% 的人口居住在占全国土地面积 57.1% 的西北部地区。

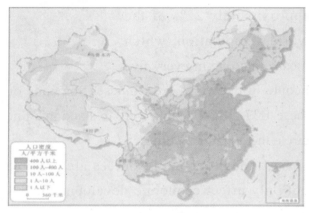

中国人口密度分布图

中国人口还有一个特点，就是农村人口多，城镇人口少。几千年来，中国一直是一个以农业经济为主的国家，绝大多数人口分布在农村，从事农业生产劳动。1949 年，中国农村人口约占全国人口的 90%，城镇人口只占 10% 多。改革开放以后，由于经济的发展，城镇人口迅速增加，到 2010 年，城镇人口占 49.68%，农村人口占 50.32%。

中国一共有 56 个民族，其中汉族是

绝大多数　juédàduōshù
overwhelming majority,
most of

城镇　chéngzhèn
cities and towns

The distribution of population in China is not at all balanced. In general, there are lots of people in the east and a few in the west. The population of the eastern coastal areas is much larger than that in the west. 94% of Chinese people dwell in southeastern China, the land area of which only accounts for 42.9% of the total land area of the country; while only approximately 6% of Chinese people live in northwestern China, the land area of which accounts for 57.1% of the entire land area.

The population of China has another characteristic: the rural population is large, while the urban population is small. Over thousands of years, China has always been a country mainly based on an agricultural economy and the majority of people are distributed in rural areas, engaging in agricultural production. In 1949, the rural population of China accounted for approximately 90% of the total population, while the urban population

在稻田里插秧的南方农民

少数民族　shǎoshù mínzú
minority ethnic group

壮族　Zhuàngzú
Zhuang ethnic group

彝族　Yízú
Yi ethnic group

藏族　Zàngzú
Tibetan ethnic group

蒙古族　Měnggǔzú
Mongolian ethnic group

信仰　xìnyǎng
belief

伊斯兰教　Yīsīlánjiào
Islam

最大的民族，占总人口的 91.51%，各少数民族人口占总人口的 8.49%。中国的少数民族包括壮族、回族、维吾尔族、彝族、苗族、满族、藏族和蒙古族等 55 个。

维吾尔族舞蹈

汉族的分布遍及全国，主要集中在东部和中部；在边疆地区，汉族多与各少数民族杂居在一起。其中，汉族有自己的语言和文字——汉语和汉字，回族和满族也使用汉语。其他的 53 个民族都有自己的语言，其中 23 个民族有自己的文字。在人民币上，除了以汉字为主要文字外，还有蒙语、维语、藏语和壮语 4 种少数民族文字。

各个民族生活的环境和条件不一样，风俗习惯也不一样。比方说，中国分布最广的少数民族回族，因为他们大多信仰伊斯兰教，所以他们的生活习惯

accounted for only more than 10%. Since China's reformation and opening up, due to economic development, the urban population has been rapidly increasing. Up to 2010, the urban population reached 49.68%, while the rural population accounted for 50.32% of the total population.

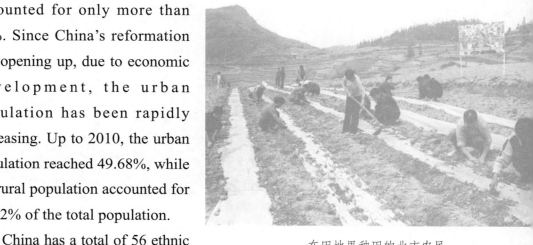

在田地里种田的北方农民

China has a total of 56 ethnic groups, of which Han ethnic group is the one with the largest population, accounting for 91.51% of the total population, and the population of all the minority ethnic groups accounts for 8.49%. Chinese minority ethnic groups include Zhuang, Hui, Uygur, Yi, Miao, Man, Tibetan and Mongolian among others, totaling 55 minority ethnic groups.

The Han people can be seen throughout China, and most of them are found in the eastern and central regions; in the frontier regions, the Han people often live together with other minority ethnic groups. Among them, the Han people have their own language and writing system, namely Mandarin and Chinese

穿着民族服饰的苗族姑娘

婴儿　yīng'ér
baby, infant

阿訇　āhōng
imam

戴　dài
to wear, to put on

宁夏银川的清真寺

受宗教影响较大，如婴儿出生要请阿訇起名字，结婚要请阿訇念泥卡哈，去世后一般要请清真寺里的教长主持葬礼；不吃猪肉、动物的血等食物；男子喜欢戴白色小帽，等等。在中国，回族一方面分布很广，另一方面有自己的聚居地。宁夏的回族人口最多，占当地总人口的 10% 以上，所以在那儿设立了宁夏回族自治区。

彝族的火把节

characters. The Hui and Man peoples also use Mandarin. Over 50 ethnic groups have their own languages, 23 of which have their own writing systems. On the bills of RMB, in addition to

人民币背面上的四种少数民族语言

Mandarin Chinese, Mongolian language, Uygur language, Tibetan language and Zhuang language can also be found.

The living environment and conditions of each ethnic group is different, so their customs also differ. Let's take the most widely distributed minority ethnic group, the Hui ethnic group, as an example, When a baby is born, an imam would be asked to give the baby a name; when a couple gets married, an imam would be asked to recite "Nikah"; when someone passes away, usually an imam from the mosque would be asked to host the funeral. They do not eat pork, nor the blood of animals among other food; men prefer to wear a white hat, etc. In China, on the one hand, Hui ethnic group is widely distributed all over the country; on the other hand, they have their own settlement. The population of Hui is the largest in Ningxia, taking up more than 10% of the local population,

清真寺里阿訇在讲经

很多少数民族还有自己的特色节日，比较知名的有蒙古族的"那达慕大会"、傣族的"泼水节"①、彝族的"火把节"、苗族的"芦笙节"，等等。

壮族服饰

尽管各个民族有不同的语言、服装、饮食习惯和节日，但是这五十六个民族都是"中华民族"这个大家庭中的兄弟姐妹。就像《爱我中华》这首歌里唱的一样："五十六个民族，五十六枝花，五十六族兄弟姐妹是一家，五十六种语言，汇成一句话：爱我中华！爱我中华！爱我中华！"

傣族　Dǎizú
Dai ethnic group

泼水节　Pōshuǐ Jié
Songkran Festival

火把节　Huǒbǎ Jié
Torch Festival

芦笙节　Lúshēng Jié
Lusheng Festival

汇成　huìchéng
to combine

云南西双版纳的傣族泼水节

56个民族的新人代表齐聚新疆天山举行盛大婚礼

therefore, Ningxia Hui Autonomous Region was established there.

A large number of minority ethnic groups also have their own festivals, the most famous ones of which include Naadam Fair of Mongolian, the Songkran (Water-Splashing) Festival of Dai, the Torch Festival of Yi, the Lusheng Festival of Miao and others.

Although each ethnic group differs in language, costume, diet and festival, the 56 ethnic groups are like brothers and sisters in the large family of Chinese nation. As the lyrics in the song *Our Love for China* says, "Like 56 flowers, the 56 ethnic groups are brothers and sisters in one family. In 56 languages, the Chinese people utter one same sentence: We love China! We love China! We love China! "

文化注释

❶ 泼水节

　　泼水节是傣族人民每年的重大节日。按照傣历，泼水节大约在清明节后的 4 月 13 日至 15 日举行。过去的习俗是头两天送旧，最后一天迎新。清晨，男女老幼沐浴更衣到佛寺"赕（dǎn）佛"（祭祀神佛），泼水嬉戏，认为这样可消灾除病。下午举行"丢包"，这是青年男女借以求爱的一种活动。现在，泼水节增加了一些新内容，第一天开庆祝会，各族同贺佳节，会后举行丰富多彩的文艺、体育表演，在江边、寨旁放高升、赛龙舟、跳孔雀舞、放孔明灯等等；次日各村寨举行泼水活动；第三天赶摆（集市贸易）。

◇练习◇

■ 阅读理解 Reading comprehension

练习 1：判断正误 Decide whether the following statements are right（ √ ）or wrong（ × ）

例　中国一共有 56 个民族，汉族是最大的民族。（ √ ）

1. 汉族的人口最多，大概占全国总人口的 60% 左右。（　　）

2. 中国人口总数达 13.7 亿，大概占世界总人口的 22%。（　　）

3. 中国人口还有一个特点，就是农村人口多。（　　）

4. 中国人口的 90% 以上居住在西部地区。（　　）

5. 中国城镇人口比重低于世界发达国家城市人口的比重。（　　）

6. 中国的 56 个民族都有自己的语言和文字。（　　）

7. 20 世纪 70 年代末，中国政府开始提倡一对夫妇只生一个孩子。（　　）

8. 少数民族中，回族分布最广，而且有自己的聚居地。（　　　）

9. "火把节"是蒙古族的风俗。（　　　）

10. 在新中国的人民币纸币上采用了四种少数民族文字。（　　　）

练习2：选择正确答案 Choose the right answers

例 中国一共有五十六个民族，_____A_____ 是最大的民族。

　　A. 汉族　　　　　B. 少数民族　　　　C. 回族　　　　D. 藏族

1. 截止到 2010 年 11 月 1 日，中国人口总数达到_____。

　　A. 13.7 亿　　　　B. 10 亿　　　　C. 11 亿　　　　D. 12 亿

2. 世界上每_____中就有 1 个中国人。

　　A. 10 个人　　　　B. 5 个人　　　　C. 22 个人　　　　D. 13 个人

3. 中国过多的人口影响了_____。

　　A. 人口的增长　　　　　　　　B. 西部人口分布

　　C. 全国土地面积　　　　　　　D. 经济的发展

4. _____有效地控制了中国人口的迅速增长。

　　A. 经济发展　　　B. 计划生育政策　　　C. 居住环境　　　D. 人口普查统计

5. 中国人口的 94% 居住在_____。

　　A. 东南部地区　　　B. 西北部地区　　　C. 高原地区　　　D. 山地

6. 在西北部地区居住的人口大概占全国总人口的_____。

　　A. 94%　　　　B. 43%　　　　C. 6%　　　　D. 57%

7. 男子喜欢戴白帽是＿＿＿＿＿＿的风俗习惯。

    A. 汉族   B. 回族   C. 蒙古族   D. 满族

8. ＿＿＿＿＿＿是蒙古族特有的风俗。

    A. 火把节   B. 泼水节   C. 那达慕大会   D. 芦笙节

9. 在新中国的人民币纸币上，＿＿＿＿＿＿采用汉字外，还有蒙、维、藏、壮四种少数民族文字。

    A. 除了   B. 还有   C. 只有   D. 因为

10. 除了回族和满族以外，其他的 50 多个少数民族都有自己的＿＿＿＿＿＿。

    A. 文字   B. 民族语言   C. 自治区   D. 沿海城镇

语段练习 Exercises about paragraphs

连线 Match the statements on the left with those on the right

1. 人口普查统计结果显示	A. 大概是世界总人口的 22%
2. 中国人口总数	B. 可以绕地球赤道 26 圈
3. 东部沿海一带的人口多于	C. 中国人口总数达到 13.7 亿
4. 世界上每 5 个人中	D. 而且对居住环境也没有好处
5. 中国人口的 94% 居住在	E. 仍有 8.6 亿多居住在农村
6. 西北部地区土地面积占	F. 有 56 个民族
7. 如果 13.7 亿中国人手拉手排成一条线	G. 就有 1 个中国人
8. 中国是一个统一的多民族的国家	H. 全国土地面积 57.1%
9. 全国 13 亿多人口中	I. 西部的人口
10. 中国过多的人口影响了经济的发展	J. 东南部地区

三 词汇练习 Exercises about vocabulary

用本课所学的新词填空 Fill in the blanks with the words in this lesson

实行	资源	风俗	提倡	尽管
杂居	信仰	知名	均衡	遍及

中国是世界上人口最多的国家。人口总数已经达到 13.7 亿，占世界总人口的 22%。虽然人力 <u>资源</u> 是宝贵的，但是过多的人口也有坏处，因此，中国_____了计划生育政策，_____一对夫妇只生一个孩子，有效地控制了人口的迅速增长。中国的人口分布很不_____，总的特点是：东多西少；农村人口多，城镇人口少。中国一共有 56 个民族，其中汉族是最大的民族，占总人口 90% 以上。其他有壮族、回族等 55 个少数民族，人口不足总人口的 10%。汉族_____全国，主要集中在东部和中部；在边疆地区，汉族多与各少数民族_____在一起。其中，汉族有自己的语言和文字——汉语和汉字，回族和满族也使用汉语。其他的 50 多个民族都有他们自己民族的语言，其中 23 个民族有他们自己的文字。各个民族有各自独特的_____习惯。比方说，回族他们大多_____伊斯兰教，生活习惯受伊斯兰教影响很大。其他比较_____的风俗，比如有蒙古族"那达慕大会"、傣族的"泼水节"、彝族的"火把节"、苗族的"芦笙节"，等等。_____各个民族的人们有各自不同的语言、服装、饮食习惯和节日，但是这 56 个民族都是"中华民族"这个大家庭中的兄弟姐妹。

四 语法练习 Exercises about grammar

用所给的词语组句 Make sentences with the words given

例　人口　中国的　大概　占　世界　总人口的　22%
　　<u>中国的人口大概占世界总人口的 22%。</u>

1. 世界　每　中国人　上　中　1个　5个　人　就　有

_____

2. 一个　中国　国家　以　为主的　是　几千年来　一直　农业经济

_____

3. 全国　中　人口　仍有　13亿多　农村　居住　在　8.6亿多

_____

4. 几乎　风俗　民族　习惯　有　都　各自　每个　独特的

_____

5. 个　民族　56　这个　都是　中的　兄弟姐妹　大家庭　"中华民族"

_____

五 写作练习 Writing practice

用下列词语造句 Make sentences using the following words and phrases

1. 截止到：_____

2. A 占 B 的百分之……：_____

3. 也就是说：_____

4. 不但……而且……：_____

5. 对……没有好处：_____

6. A 多于 B：_____

7. 大概：_____

8. 绝大多数：_____

9. 一方面……，另一方面……：_____

10. 尽管……，但是……：_____

中国的气候和南北文化

4

大雪之后的北京箭扣长城

1. 你知道北京除了上图中的箭扣长城还有那些长城吗？
2. 中国气候（climate）的特点是什么？
3. 东南风和西北风是从哪儿刮（to blow）来的？它们对气候有什么影响？
4. 北方人和南方人吃的食物（food）跟气候有什么关系？
5. 如果你选择住在中国，你想住在什么地方？为什么？

中国国土面积广大，所以不同地方的气候差别很大。

中国气候的特点之一是：冬季气温普遍偏低，南热北冷，南北温差很大；夏季南北普遍高温，南北温差不大。

冬季南北温差大的主要原因是：冬季太阳直射南半球，北半球获得太阳能量少，另外，受纬度影响，冬季盛行冬季风，所以北方大部分地区气温低。同时，中国南北温度相差50℃，所以南北温差很大。比如春节的时候，位于东北的哈尔滨冰天雪地、雪花飘飘，而南方的广州却是阳光明媚、鲜花盛开；当北方的孩子在冰天雪地里打雪仗、滑冰、滑雪的时候，南方的人们却在温暖的海水里游泳呢。

春节买年花的广州市民

北方的冬天虽然寒冷，但风景却很

国土	guótǔ
territory	
气候	qìhòu
climate	
差别	chābié
difference	
冬季	dōngjì
winter	
普遍	pǔbiàn
general	
温差	wēnchā
difference in temperature	
夏季	xiàjì
summer	
能量	néngliàng
energy	
纬度	wěidù
latitude	
飘	piāo
to flutter	
明媚	míngmèi
bright and beautiful	
鲜花	xiānhuā
(fresh) flower	
盛开	shèngkāi
to bloom	
滑冰	huá bīng
to skate	
滑雪	huá xuě
to ski	
温暖	wēnnuǎn
warm	

China has vast territory, so the climate in different regions varies greatly.

One of the characteristics of China's climate is that the temperature is generally low in winter and differs greatly from the north to the south, with the temperature of the south higher than that of the north. It is generally hot in summer and the temperature differs slightly from the north to the south.

东北的冬天特有的雾凇景观

The main reason accounting for the big difference in temperature between northern and southern China is that the southern hemisphere is directly exposed to sunshine, and the northern hemisphere receives little solar energy in winter. Besides, under the effect of latitude, wind often blows in winter, so it is cold in most northern areas. Meanwhile, the latitude in China varies 50℃ from the north to the south, therefore the temperature differs greatly. For instance, in Spring Festival, Harbin

北京附近滑雪场里滑雪的小朋友

冰封　bīng fēng
icebound

写照　xiězhào
portrayal

度假　dù jià
to take a vacation

溜冰　liū bīng
to skate

观赏　guānshǎng
to watch (with appreciation)

雕　diāo
to carve

相对　xiàngduì
relatively

美，"北国风光，千里冰封，万里雪飘"就是对北方冬天冰雪飘零的壮美风光的写照。很多人喜欢冬天到中国的北方旅游度假，滑雪、溜冰，到哈尔滨观赏一年一度的冰灯冰雕展①，非常有趣。长

冰块雕成的建筑

江以南的上海、南京等城市，冬天也很冷，但是相对来说，比北方要温暖得多，广东、广西等地方，冬天则很暖和，一年四季树木都是绿的。

春节时的广州花草树木都是绿的

of northeast China is covered with ice and snow everywhere and snowflakes are fluttering, while Guangzhou of southern China has bright sunshine and blooming flowers. When kids in northern China are playing with snowballs, skating or skiing, southern Chinese are swimming in warm sea water.

Although winter in northern China is cold, the scenery there is beautiful. The poem "northern China is icebound for thousands of miles and has snowflakes fluttering for ten thousands of miles" portrays the splendid scenery in the winter of northern China. Many people like to go to northern China in winter on their vacation to ski, skate, watch the annual Ice Lamp or Ice Sculpture Shows in Harbin. Although it is

虎年春节期间广州街头鲜花盛开

also cold in winter in cities south of Yangtze River, such as Shanghai and Nanjing, it is much warmer there than in northern cities, especially in places such as Guangdong and Guangxi, where trees are green all year round.

In general, summer is hot in China and the temperature doesn't differ greatly from the north to the south. It is mainly because the northern hemisphere is directly exposed to sunshine and gets more heat in summer. Wind often blows in summer, and the temperature rises to its maximum in most areas of China. The sun rises high up in the sky. The higher the latitude is, the longer the daytime is, the longer the sun shines, and the smaller

北半球　běibànqiú
northern hemisphere

热量　rèliàng
heat, quantity of heat

减缓　jiǎnhuǎn
to slow down

差异　chāyì
difference

昼夜　zhòuyè
day and night

皮袄　pí'ǎo
fur coat

纱　shā
gauze, yarn

火炉　huǒlú
stove

西瓜　xīguā
watermelon

新疆　Xīnjiāng
Xingjiang Uyghur
Autonomous Region
located in northwest China

早晚　zǎowǎn
day and night

漠河　Mòhé
a town in the northernmost
of China

吐鲁番　Tǔlǔfān
Turpan

中国的夏季普遍高温，南北温差不大，主要原因在于：夏季太阳直射北半球，北半球获得热量多；夏季盛行夏季风，中国大部分地区气温上升到最高值；夏季太阳高度大，纬度越高，白天时间越长，日照时间也就越长，减缓了南北接受太阳光热的差异。虽然南北温差不大，但是东西部的昼夜温差却有很大差异：东部昼夜温差小，西部昼夜温差大。"早穿皮袄午穿纱，抱着火炉吃西瓜"，说的就是夏天的新疆白天很热，需要穿很薄的衣服，而早晚却很冷，需要穿很厚的衣服。

黑龙江漠河的冬天

中国冬季最冷的地方是黑龙江的漠河镇，夏季最热的地方是吐鲁番，不过重庆、武汉、南京夏季也很热，号称中国"三大火炉"。

difference in the quantity of sunshine the north and the south get. Although the temperature doesn't differ greatly from the north to the south, the temperature of the day and night differs greatly in the east and the west. In eastern China, the temperature of the day and night varies slightly, but it is just the other way around in western China. The

哈尔滨的冰雕

saying "wearing a fur coat in the morning and gauze at noon, and eating watermelon while sitting around the stove to keep warm" indicates that Xinjiang is hot in summer during the day, so people need to wear very light clothes; but it is cold at night, so people have to wear very heavy clothes.

The coldest place in China in winter is the town of Mohe and the hottest place in summer is Turpan. However, Chongqing, Wuhan and Nanjing also have a hot summer and are known as China's "Three Big Stoves".

The second characteristic of Chinese climate is that it has much precipitation in summer and little in winter. The total precipitation

新疆喀什集市风光

降水　jiàngshuǐ
rainfall, precipitation

逐渐　zhújiàn
gradually

湿润　shīrùn
moist

海洋　hǎiyáng
ocean

季风　jìfēng
monsoon

几乎　jīhū
almost

梅雨　méiyǔ
Plum Rain Season (or "East Asian Rainy Season")

植物　zhíwù
plant

寒冷　hánlěng
cold

稀薄　xībó
thin

氧气　yǎngqì
oxygen

高原反应　gāoyuán fǎnyìng
altitude sickness

中国气候的特点之二是：夏季降水多，冬季降水少；总降水量从东南向西北逐渐减少。其原因在于：夏季温暖又湿润的海洋季风从海上吹来，会带来雨水，所以在江南，有些地区每年6月～7月几乎每天都在下雨，人们把这段时间叫作"梅雨季节"。而中国西部离海洋很远，带着降雨的海洋季风很难影响到西部，所以很少下雨，植物也比东边少得多。而到了冬天，受寒冷干燥的西北风影响，大部分地区都比较寒冷、干燥。

南方水田中的水稻

青藏高原的气候是比较特别的，因为海拔高，所以日照特别强，空气稀薄，氧气少。很多去那儿旅游的人都不适应，常常出现高原反应，如果你想去西藏旅游，一定要提前做好准备。

南北气候上的差异还影响了人们的

中国最美丽的乡村婺源（位于江西）

gradually decreases from the southeast to the northwest. It is because that the warm and moist marine monsoon blowing in summer causes rainfall. As a result, in June and July every year, some areas in south of Yangtze River have rainfalls almost every day. This period of time is thus known as the "Plum Rain Season (or "East Asian Rainy Season"). Since western China is very far away from the sea, it is almost impossible to be affected by the marine monsoon; therefore, it seldom rains there and there are much fewer plants than in the east. In winter, under the northwest wind, most areas of western China are rather cold and dry.

The climate in Qinghai-Tibet Plateau is very special. The high elevation causes strong sunshine, thin air and oxygen deficiency; so many tourists are not accustomed to the climate there, often having altitude sickness. If you want to go there, you'd better be well prepared.

Difference in climate between the south and the north results in a variety of people's lifestyles. For example, what northerners eat is

食物	shíwù	food
耕地	gēngdì	arable land
旱	hàn	drought
适合	shìhé	suitable
耐寒	nài hán	

cold-resistant

小麦	xiǎomài	wheat
养成	yǎngchéng	

to develop (a habit)

面食	miànshí	

cooked wheaten food

水稻	shuǐdào	rice
主食	zhǔshí	staple food
选择	xuǎnzé	

to select, to choose

低度	dīdù	low-alcohol
节奏	jiézòu	rhythm, pace
缓慢	huǎnmàn	slow
含蓄	hánxù	implicit
委婉	wěiwǎn	

euphemistic

台风	táifēng	typhoon
龙卷风	lóngjuǎnfēng	

tornado

飓风	jùfēng	hurricane
人文	rénwén	humanity
地理	dìlǐ	geography
享受	xiǎngshòu	to enjoy
惊喜	jīngxǐ	

pleasant surprise

乐趣	lèqù	fun, joy

生活习惯。比如，北方人和南方人吃的食物不太一样。北方降水较少，气温较低，因此耕地多为旱地，适合喜干耐寒的小麦生长，时间久了，北方人就养成了喜欢吃面食的习惯。而南方的气候湿润多雨，耕地多以水田为主，适合喜高温多雨的水稻，于是南方人就以米为主食。在对酒的选择上，北方人偏好老白干、二锅头等高度烈酒，喜欢大碗喝酒大口吃肉，豪放洒脱，这和北方寒冷的气候有关；而南方人则热衷于米酒等低度酒，而且他们生活节奏相对缓慢，性格含蓄，说话委婉。

北方旱地里的麦子

总体来说，中国的气候还是非常宜人的，台风、龙卷风和飓风比较少。欢迎你来中国游学、旅行，亲身体验中国大江南北不同的气候、人文地理和风土人情，享受春夏秋冬四季变化的惊喜和乐趣。

not exactly the same as those of the southerners. Since northern China is characterized by less precipitation and low temperature and there are mostly dry lands, which are suitable for the cold-resistant wheat to grow. As time passes, northerners have developed a liking for cooked wheaten food. While southern

河北省塞罕坝的夏天

China is characterized by humid climate and there are mostly paddy fields, which are suitable for rice to grow. As a result, rice is the staple food for southerners. In choice of liquor, northerners prefor hard liquor such as Laobaigan and Erguotou, and like to drink with big glasses and eat big pieces of meat, all of which are related to the cold climate in northern China. In contrast, southerners like to drink low-alcohol liquor such as rice wine; with a slower life pace, they have a implicit character and euphemistic way of speaking.

Generally speaking, China has a very pleasant climate and is seldom hit by a typhoon, tornado or hurricane. Welcome to study/travel in China. You'll experience its different climates, humanity, geography and local customs, while enjoying the surprises and fun in the change of seasons.

西藏雅鲁藏布江春天的风光

文化注释

❶ 哈尔滨冰雕节

又称哈尔滨国际冰雪节，是中国历史上第一个以冰雪活动为内容的国际性节日，开始时间是每年 1 月 5 日，根据天气状况和活动安排，持续时间为一个月左右，与日本札幌雪节、加拿大魁北克冬季狂欢节和挪威滑雪节并称世界四大冰雪节。

冰雪节期间会举办冬泳比赛、冰球赛、雪地足球赛、高山滑雪邀请赛、国际冰雕比赛、冰上速滑赛、冰雪节诗会、冰雪摄影展、图书展、冰雪电影艺术节、冰上婚礼等多种活动。

◇ 练习 ◇

一 阅读理解 Reading comprehension

练习 1：判断正误 Decide whether the following statements are right（ √ ）or wrong（ × ）

例 中国国土面积广大，但是气候差别却不大。（ √ ）

1. 中国气候的特点之一是：夏季南北温差很大。（　　）

2. 春节的时候，哈尔滨是冰天雪地，而广州却是阳光明媚。（　　）

3. 中国西部离海洋很远，所以一年四季很少下雨。（　　）

4. 新疆地处中国西部，所以夏天温差很大。（　　）

5. 冬季风的特点是温暖湿润。（　　）

6. 西北风从中国西北边的内陆吹过来，带来降水。（　　）

7. 青藏高原因为地势高，所以空气稀薄，氧气少。（　　）

8. 中国大多数南方人都喜欢吃面食。（　　）

9. 冰灯、冰雕展每年都会在北京举行。（　　　）

10. 广东一年四季树木都是绿的。（　　　）

例 中国国土面积广大，所以不同地方 ___B___ 。

    A. 普遍高温　　　B. 气候差别很大　　　C. 冰天雪地　　　D. 阳光明媚

1. 江南的有些地区每年 6 月～ 7 月几乎天天都在下雨，这段时间被叫
作 _____ 。

    A. 梅雨季节　　　B. 高原反应　　　C. 空气稀薄　　　D. 四季分明

2. 很多人喜欢到哈尔滨观赏一年一度的 _____ 。

    A. 温暖的海里游泳　　　　　　B. 东南风

    C. 冰灯、冰雕展　　　　　　　D. 鲜花盛开

3. 夏季的海洋季风的特点是 _____ 。

    A. 寒冷又干燥　　　　　　　　B. 温暖又湿润

    C. 寒冷又湿润　　　　　　　　D. 炎热又干燥

4. 中国冬季最冷的地方是 _____ 。

    A. 武汉　　　B. 南京　　　C. 吐鲁番　　　D. 漠河镇

5. 由于北方 _____ ，因此北方人养成了喜欢吃面食的习惯。

    A. 适合小麦生长　　　　　　　B. 农作物是水稻

    C. 地势高　　　　　　　　　　D. 刮西北风

6. 因为青藏高原 _____ ，所以日照特别强，空气稀薄，氧气少。

    A. 温差大　　　B. 海拔高　　　C. 降水较少　　　D. 高温多雨

7. 春节时，当北方的孩子们滑冰、滑雪的时候，南方的广州人却_____。

    A. 晚抱火炉吃西瓜　　　　　　　　B. 大碗喝酒大口吃肉

    C. 出现高原反应　　　　　　　　　D. 在温暖的海水里游泳呢

8. 北方人偏好_____，这和北方的冬季比南方更冷有关。

    A. 梅雨季节　　　B. 米酒　　　　　C. 西北风　　　　D. 高度烈酒

9. 南方的气候_____，耕地多以水田为主，适合种植水稻。

    A. 高温多雨　　　B. 降水较少　　　C. 气温较低　　　D. 温差较大

10. "早穿皮袄午穿纱，抱着火炉吃西瓜"，说的是_____夏季的气候特点。

    A. 广东　　　　　B. 哈尔滨　　　　C. 新疆　　　　　D. 青藏高原

语段练习 Exercises about paragraphs

连线 Match the statements on the left with those on the right

1. 中国国土面积广大，所以　　　　　A. 一个月的时间几乎每天都在下雨

2. 北方人和南方人吃的食物　　　　　B. 适合喜干耐寒的小麦生长

3. 很多人喜欢冬天到中国的北方　　　C. 不同地方的气候差别很大

4. 江南"梅雨"季节的时候　　　　　D. 老白干、二锅头等高度烈酒

5. 北方降水较少，所以适合　　　　　E. 相对缓慢，性格相对含蓄

6. 南方的气候湿润多雨，因而耕地　　F. 植物比东边少得多

7. 在对酒的选择上，北方人偏好　　　G. 很大程度上是受气候的影响

8. 南方人生活节奏　　　　　　　　　H. 北半球获得的热量多

9. 西部不常下雨，因此　　　　　　　I. 旅游度假，滑雪、溜冰

10. 夏季太阳直射北半球　　　　　　　J. 多以水田为主

三 词汇练习 Exercises about vocabulary

用本课所学的新词填空 Fill in the blanks with the words in this lesson

主食	差异	逐渐	湿润	气候
普遍	盛行	养成	适合	干燥

　　因为中国的国土面积很大，所以各个地区的　气候　都不太一样，有着自己的特点。中国气温的总的分布特点是：冬季气温＿＿＿＿＿＿偏低，南热北冷，南北温差很大；夏季南北普遍高温，温差不大。主要原因在于：夏季太阳直射北半球，＿＿＿＿＿＿夏季风，白昼时间长。中国降水的分布特点是：夏季降水多，冬季降水少；总降水量从东南向西北＿＿＿＿＿＿减少。原因在于：夏季温暖又＿＿＿＿＿＿的海洋季风从海上吹来，会带来雨水。而中国西部离海洋很远，带着降雨的季风很难影响到西部，所以西部不常下雨。而冬天到了后，中国大部分地区受寒冷、＿＿＿＿＿＿的西北风影响，所以冬天的气候大部分地区比较寒冷、干燥。南北气候上的＿＿＿＿＿＿也影响到北方人和南方人吃的食物。由于北方降水较少，气温较低，＿＿＿＿＿＿喜干耐寒的小麦生长，因此北方人＿＿＿＿＿＿了喜欢吃面食的习惯。而南方的气候高温多雨，耕地多以水田为主，适合喜高温多雨的水稻，于是南方人则以米为＿＿＿＿＿＿。

四 语法练习 Exercises about grammar

用所给的词语组句 Make sentences with the words given

例　不同地方的　中国　气候　所以　很大　国土面积　差别　广大

　　中国国土面积广大，所以不同地方的气候差别很大。

1. 稀薄　日照　地势高　所以　特别强　空气　青藏高原

_____

2. 冬天　中国的　旅游度假　喜欢　到　滑雪　溜冰　很多人　北方

_____

3. 去那儿　很多　不适应　旅游的人　那儿的气候　出现　常常　高原反应

_____

4. 耕地　水田　多　为主　以　水稻　喜高温　多雨的　适合

_____

5. 北方人　和　吃的食物　南方人　不太一样

_____

五 写作练习 Writing practice

用下列词语造句 **Make sentences using the following words and phrases**

1. 普遍：_____

2. 受……的影响：_____

3. 鲜花盛开：_____

4. 虽然……但是…… ：_____

5. ……的写照：_____

6. 几乎：_____

7. 养成了……的习惯：_____

8. 以……为主：_____

9. 和……有关：_____

10. 热衷于：_____

陕西的西岳华山以"险"著称

导读问题　Lead-in questions

1. 你去过上图中的山吗？
2. 你能讲述中国神话故事里关于"三山"的传说吗？
3. "重如泰山"和"稳如泰山"是什么意思？
4. 现在人们到山东旅游，为什么一般都会去爬泰山？
5. 爬山有什么好处？为什么人们对"三山五岳"都十分向往？

提起 tíqǐ
to mention, to speak of

著名 zhùmíng
famous

岳 yuè
high mountain

蓬莱 Pénglái
name of a legendary mountain

方丈 Fāngzhàng
name of a legendary mountain

瀛洲 Yíngzhōu
name of a legendary mountain

衡山 Héng Shān
Mt. Heng in Hunan

恒山 Héng Shān
Mt. Heng in Shanxi

嵩山 Sōng Shān
Mt. Song in Henan

神话 shénhuà
iyth, mythology

传说 chuánshuō
legend

神仙 shénxiān
immortal being

皇帝 huángdì
emperor

派 pài
to send

寻找 xúnzhǎo
to look for, to find

提起中国著名的大山，不得不说"三山五岳"。这里的"三山"指的是传说中的蓬莱、方丈和瀛洲三山，五岳指的是东岳泰山、南岳衡山、西岳华山、北岳恒山和中岳嵩山。

山东威海蓬莱阁风光

蓬莱、方丈和瀛洲是中国神话故事中的三座山。传说在中国东边大海里有三座山，山上住着神仙。这里有一种药，人们吃了之后也会变成神仙，不会变老。古时候有很多人相信这个传说，特别是一些皇帝，他们希望自己能长生不老，永远管理自己的国家，所以就派很多人去寻找这三座山，希望找到长生不老的药。事实上，这一切只是神话传说，不是真的，没有人找到过这三座住着神仙的山。现在的蓬莱是中国的一个沿海城市，被人们称为"人间仙境"，传说，八仙过海的故事就发生在这里。

Speaking of famous Chinese mountains, the following eight ones are noteworthy, the "Three *Shan*" and the "Five *Yue*". The "Three *Shan* (mountain)" refer to the three legendary mountains, Penglai, Fangzhang and Yingzhou; the "Five *Yue* (high Mountains)" refer to Mount

蓬莱景区里的八仙过海雕塑

Tai in the east, Mount Heng in the south, Mount Hua in the west, Mount Heng in the north and Mount Song in the east in Central China.

Penglai, Fangzhang and Yingzhou are three mountains in the sea to the east of China in Chinese mythology. Legends say that immortal beings live on these mountains. A kind of medicine can be found there, which makes one never grow old and become an immortal, too. Many ancient Chinese, especially emperors, believed this legend was true. The emperors hoped they would have an everlasting life and always be the state ruler, so they sent many people to search the three mountains, hoping to find the elixir of life. In fact, these are just legends. Nobody can found these mountains. Known as the "fairyland on earth", the present-day Penglai is a Chinese

东岳泰山

coastal city, where eight immortals were said to cross the sea.

坐落　zuòluò
to be situated, to be located

祭拜　jìbài
to hold a memorial
ceremony, to worship

热门　rèmén
hot, popular

胜地　shèngdì
resort

海拔　hǎibá　altitude

英尺　yīngchǐ
foot (≈ 0.348 meter)

雄伟　xióngwěi
majestic

挺拔　tǐngbá
upright

平原　píngyuán
plain

因而　yīn'ér
thus

视觉　shìjué
vision

格外　géwài
exceptionally

连绵　liánmián
rolling

雄浑　xiónghún
forceful

壮美　zhuàngměi
magnificent and beautiful

说法　shuōfǎ
statement, wording, saying

　　五岳的岳是"高大的山"的意思，五岳就是五座高山。因为这五座山坐落在中国五个不同的地方，按照方位，被人们称为：东岳、南岳、西岳、北岳和中岳。

东岳泰山的云海

　　在中国古代，五岳是皇帝祭拜天地的地方。现在这五座山都是非常热门的旅游胜地。其中最有名的是东岳泰山，它位于山东省中部泰安市，主峰海拔1545米（大约5068英尺）。在中国的大山中，这个高度仅排在第16位，但它却被称为"五岳之首"，这是为什么呢？原来泰山雄伟挺拔，坐落在一片平原中央，在数百公里内，只有它这一座高山，因而在视觉上显得格外高大。泰山山脉连绵100多公里，给人以雄浑、壮美的感觉，所以有"重如泰山"（形容某件事作用和价值非常大）、"稳如泰山"（像泰山一样稳重）的说法。

In ancient China, emperors offered sacrifices to heaven and earth on the Five Mountains, all of which are now popular tourist destinations. The most famous one is Mount Tai in the east. It is situated in Tai'an City of mid-Shandong Province with its highest peak being 1545 meters (approximately 5068 feet) above sea level. Of Chinese mountains, Mount Tai only ranks the 16th in height, but why is it the most revered of the five high mountains? Mount Tai looks exceptionally upright because it stands majestically in the middle of a plain and is the only mountain within hundreds of

泰山石刻

kilometers. Impressing people visually with its majesty and grandeur, the mountain range of Mount Tai stretches over 100 kilometers, thus the sayings "as heavy as Mount Tai" (indicating something has very important function and value) and "as steady as Mount Tai".

Many emperors worshipped and attached much importance to Mount Tai. Starting from the first emperor of Qin, such worship had been performed for over thousands of years in almost all the Chinese dynasties. Of all the Chinese mountains, Mount Tai is the only one that has a central axis ascending from the foot of the mountain to its top, which is 9 kilometers in total length with over 6000 steps. In the eyes of ancient Chinese, this staircase linked the

远观泰山十八盘

延续　yánxù
to continue

中轴线　zhōngzhóuxiàn
central axis

天堂　tiāntáng
heaven, paradise

朝代　cháodài
dynasty

建筑　jiànzhù
architecture

和睦　hémù
harmonious

儒家　Rújiā
Confucianism

道教　Dàojiào
Taoism

佛教　Fójiào
Buddhism

寺庙　sìmiào
temple

展示　zhǎnshì
to show, to display

包容　bāoróng
tolerance

赞美　zànměi
to praise

抒发　shūfā
to express

一览众山小
yì lǎn zhòng shān xiǎo
to hold all mountains in a single glance

　　泰山还受到过很多帝王的朝拜和重视。从秦始皇开始，这种朝拜延续了数千年，几乎贯串中国的各个朝代。在中国所有的山中，只有泰山有一条从山下直通山顶的中轴线，这条中轴线全长约9公里，有6000多台阶。在古代人眼中，这个天梯连接了人间与天堂。另外，泰山还有各个朝代建的古建筑近百处。在这里，不同宗教和睦相处，有儒家的祠堂、道教的宫观，还有佛教的寺庙等，展示了泰山的博大与包容。从古到今，很多文学家都以诗词文章等形式来赞美

泰山上的佛教寺庙

泰山，抒发他们对泰山的崇敬喜爱。现在人们到山东旅游一般都会去爬泰山，到泰山顶上观看日出，体验"一览众山小"①的感觉。

　　南岳衡山在湖南省，衡山到处都

earth and heaven. Furthermore, there are nearly 100 ancient buildings on Mount Tai built in different dynasties, including the Confucian ancestral hall, the Taoist temples and Buddhist temples. All the religions have been harmoniously co-existing here, showing the broadness and tolerance of Mount Tai. Since

泰山孔子庙

ancient times, many literati have always been writing poems and articles to praise Mount Tai, expressing their respect and love for it. Nowadays, if people travel to Shandong, they usually ascend Mount Tai. When they are watching the sunrise at the top of it, they feel all the other mountains are so small.

The beautiful Mount Heng in the south, located in Hunan Province, is densely covered with trees and has the shades of trees and the fragrance of flowers all year round. The Mount Hua in the west, located in Shaanxi Province, is very precipitous due to the narrow paths and high steps on it. So,

泰山道教岱庙

please be careful when you climb it. But just because of its precipitousness

芬芳	fēnfāng	
fragrant		
秀丽	xiùlì	
beautifulous, precipitous		
险	xiǎn	
danger		
悬空寺	Xuánkōng Sì	
Hanging Temple		
巨人	jùrén	
giant		
少林寺	Shàolín Sì	
Shaolin Temple (in Henan)		

高峰	gāofēng	
peak		
领略	lǐnglüè	
to appreciate		
雄姿	xióngzī	
majestic appearance		
和谐	héxié	
harmonious		
流连忘返	liúlián wàngfǎn	
to linger on		

是树木，一年四季都绿树成荫，花草芬芳，十分秀丽；西岳华山在陕西省，华山非常险，上山的路很窄，台阶很高，爬山的时候要特别注意安全。也正是因为华山的险，所以很多爬山爱好者都喜欢来这里登山、探险；山西省的北岳恒山是五岳中最高的山，恒山半山的悬崖上有一个寺庙，看上去好像建在空中，所以叫作悬空寺，很有特色；中岳嵩山在河南省，嵩山不高，但是范围很广，像一位巨人平躺在那里一样。著名的少林寺②就在嵩山。

河南嵩山少林寺

中国的三山五岳各具特色，很受人们的喜爱。如果你到中国旅行，虽然传说中的蓬莱、方丈和瀛洲三座仙山是找不到的，但是你可以到五岳去攀登高峰，领略它们的雄姿，体验那里的历史、文化与自然的和谐共处，你一定会流连忘返。

and steepness. it attracts many mountain climbers to climb it, enjoying their adventurous experience on it. Mount Heng in the north, located in Shanxi Province, is the highest of the five mountains. A temple hanging halfway on the mountain slope seems to be built in mid-air, so it is known as the Hanging Temple. The Mount Song

山西恒山悬空寺

in Central China sits in Henan Province. Although it is not high, it covers a wide range and looks like a giant lying there. The famous Shaolin Temple is located on Mount Song.

Each of the legendary Three Mountains and Five High Mountains of China is unique in its own way and all of them are loved by many people. If you travel in China, though you cannot find Penglai, Fangzhang or Yingzhou, you could certainly go to climb the Five High Mountains, enjoying their grandeur, learning their history and

陡峭险峻的西岳华山

experiencing the harmonious co-existence of culture and nature.

文化注释

❶ 一览众山小

出自唐代诗人杜甫的古诗《望岳》，"会当凌绝顶，一览众山小"。意思是：我一定要登上泰山的顶峰，俯瞰众山，而众山就会显得极为渺小。形容泰山很高，其他山都很难与之相比。

❷ 少林寺

位于中国河南省登封市嵩山五乳峰下的一座佛寺，是少林武术的发源地、汉传佛教禅宗祖庭，由于坐落于嵩山的腹地少室山下的茂密丛林中，所以取名"少林寺"。少林寺因少林功夫而名扬天下，号称"天下第一名刹"。2007 年"少林寺景区"被授予中国国家 5A 级旅游景区。2010 年 8 月 1 日，少林寺被列为世界文化遗产。

◇ 练习 ◇

▊ 阅读理解 Reading comprehension

练习 1：判断正误 Decide whether the following statements are right（ √ ）or wrong（ × ）

例 中国著名的三山指的是蓬莱、方丈和瀛洲。（ √ ）

1. 传说蓬莱、方丈和瀛洲在中国东边大海。（　　）

2. 人们对这三座山感到好奇，是因为他们是中国最高的山。（　　）

3. 中国的五岳坐落在中国五个不同的地方。（　　）

4. 衡山在中国的南边，所以就被叫作南岳。（　　）

5. 在中国群山中，泰山是最高的山，被称为"五岳之首"。（　　）

6. 在中国古代，五岳是皇帝祭拜天地的地方。（　　）

7. 南岳衡山非常秀美，一年四季花草芬芳。（　　　）

8. 西岳华山的特点是非常险，没有上山的路。（　　　）

9. 南岳衡山坐落在山西省。（　　　）

10. 著名的少林寺就在河南省的嵩山。（　　　）

练习2：选择正确答案 Choose the right answers

例 传说中的 ＿＿B＿＿ 指的是蓬莱、方丈和瀛洲。

　　A. 五岳　　　　B. 三山　　　　C. 著名大山　　　D. 最高的山

1. 传说在中国＿＿＿＿＿＿有三座山，山上住着神仙。

　　A. 东边大海里　　　　　　B. 西边平原

　　C. 南边湖南省　　　　　　D. 山西省

2. 古时候有很多人相信能在中国的三山里找到＿＿＿＿＿＿＿。

　　A. 儒家的祠堂　　　　　　B. 道教的宫观

　　C. 佛教的寺庙　　　　　　D. 长生不老的药

3. 五岳中最有名的是＿＿＿＿＿＿＿。

　　A. 衡山　　　　B. 泰山　　　　C. 华山　　　　D. 嵩山

4. 泰山被称为"五岳之首"，是因为＿＿＿＿＿＿＿。

　　A. 雄伟挺拔　　B. 住着神仙　　C. 最秀美的山　　D. 神话中的山

5. 东岳泰山位于山东省中部，周围是＿＿＿＿＿＿＿。

　　A. 一片平原　　B. 悬空寺　　　C. 中轴线　　　　D. 天梯

6. 嵩山不高，但是范围很广，像＿＿＿＿＿＿＿一样。

　　A. 一位巨人平躺在那里　　　B. 一览众山小的感觉

　　C. 6000 多层天梯　　　　　D. 古建筑群

7. 山西省的北岳_____是五岳中最高的山。

    A. 衡山　　　　B. 嵩山　　　　C. 华山　　　　　　D. 恒山

8. 华山坐落在陕西省，因而被称为_____。

    A. 西岳　　　　B. 南岳　　　　C. 中岳　　　　　　D. 北岳

9. 著名的少林寺就在河南省的_____。

    A. 泰山　　　　B. 嵩山　　　　C. 华山　　　　　　D. 恒山

10. 在古代人眼中，泰山的 6000 多层天梯连接了_____。

    A. 祠堂与宫观　　　　　　　B. 人间与天堂

    C. 东岳与西岳　　　　　　　D. 平原与高原

语段练习 Exercises about paragraphs

连线 **Match the statements on the left with those on the right**

1. 中国著名的三山指的是	A. 中国五个不同的地方
2. 岳的意思是	B. 东岳泰山
3. 中国的五岳坐落在	C. 都绿树成荫，十分秀丽
4. 在中国古代，五岳是	D. 蓬莱、方丈和瀛洲
5. 五岳中最有名、最重要的是	E. 一个悬空寺
6. 因为华山很险，所以	F. 像一位巨人平躺在那里一样
7. 在中国所有的山中，只有泰山才有	G. 高大的山
8. 南岳衡山在湖南省，一年四季	H. 受到很多爬山爱好者的喜爱
9. 北岳恒山在半山的悬崖上有	I. 一条从山下直通山顶的中轴线
10. 中岳嵩山	J. 皇帝祭拜天地的地方

三 词汇练习 Exercises about vocabulary

用本课所学的新词填空 Fill in the blanks with the words in this lesson

秀丽	平原	延续	视觉	雄伟挺拔
范围	悬崖	展示	包容	和睦相处

中国的五岳是人所共知的五座高大的山。它们是东岳泰山，西岳华山，南岳衡山，北岳恒山和中岳嵩山。先说说东岳泰山。这五座山中，最有名、最重要的是位于山东省中部泰安市的东岳泰山，它 雄伟挺拔，坐落在一片_____中央。在数百公里内，只有它这一座高山，因而在_____上显得格外高大，被称为"五岳之首"。各个朝代的帝王都到泰山朝拜，这种朝拜_____了数千年。另外，泰山还有各个朝代建的古建筑近百处。在这里，不同宗教_____，有儒家的祠堂、道教的宫观，还有佛教的寺庙等，_____了泰山的博大与_____。再说说西岳华山，它位于陕西省，上山的路很窄，台阶很高。因为华山很险，所以受到很多爬山爱好者的喜爱。南岳衡山在湖南省，到处都是树木，一年四季都绿树成荫，十分_____。山西省的北岳恒山是五岳中最高的山。在半山的_____上有一个寺庙，这座寺庙就好像建在空中，所以叫作悬空寺。最后说说河南省的中岳嵩山，嵩山不高，但是_____很广，像一位巨人平躺在那里一样。著名的少林寺就在嵩山。

四 语法练习 Exercises about grammar

用所给的词语组句 Make sentences with the words given

例 中国著名的　提起　大山　"三山五岳"　不得不说

提起中国著名的大山，不得不说"三山五岳"。

1. 住着　在　里　中国东边　有　大海　三座山　山上　神仙　传说

_____

2. 找到　没有人　过　三座　这　神仙的山　住　着

_____

3. 各个朝代　延续了　几乎　这种朝拜　贯串　中国的　数千年

_____

4. 在　眼中　连接了　这个天梯　天堂　古代人　与　人间

_____

5. 爬山爱好者的　受到　很多　华山　喜爱　因为　所以　很险

_____

五 写作练习 Writing practice

用下列词语造句 Make sentences using the following words and phrases

1. 提起……，不得不说…… ：_____

2. 雄伟挺拔：_____

3. 事实上：_____

4. 受到………的重视：_____

5. 在……眼中：_____

6. 和睦相处：_____

7. 体验……的感觉：_____

8. 绿树成荫：_____

9. 各具特色：_____

10. 流连忘返：_____

长江、黄河

美丽壮观的长江三峡

导读问题　Lead-in questions

1. 你知道上面的长江三峡位于什么地方吗？
2. 长江有多长？流经多少个省、市和自治区（autonomous region）？
3. 为什么说长江是中国东西的水上交通大动脉？
4. 为什么黄河被誉为（tobe well-known as）母亲河？
5. 长江和黄河对中国的经济发展有什么作用？

遥远	yáoyuǎn	remote
神游	shényóu	
to feel as if one were visiting a place		
澎湃	péngpài	surging
汹涌	xiōngyǒng	turbulent
横卧	héng wò	
to lie, to recline		
吸引	xīyǐn	to attract
传说	chuánshuō	legend
人间	rénjiān	the world
大旱	dàhàn	
severe drought		
拯救	zhěngjiù	to save

亚洲	Yàzhōu	Asia
青藏高原		
Qīng-Zàng Gāoyuán		
Qinghai-Tibet Plateau		
西藏	Xīzàng	Tibet
安徽	Ānhuī	
Anhui, name of a province		
自治区	zìzhìqū	
autonomous region		
流入	liúrù	to flow into
全长	quáncháng	
total length		
名副其实	míngfùqíshí	
to be worthy of the name		

有这样一首歌："遥远的东方有一条江，它的名字叫长江；遥远的东方有一条河，它的名字叫黄河。谁不曾看见长江美，梦里常神游长江水；谁不曾听见黄河壮，澎湃汹涌在梦里……"

打开中国地图，你一定会被地图上巨龙一般横卧着的两条大河所吸引——这就是长江和黄河。传说长江、黄河本来是天上的两条龙，它们看到人间大旱，为了拯救人类，便化为两条大河，留在了人间。

冰雪覆盖的唐古拉山，是长江的发源地

长江是亚洲第一长河，也是世界第三长河，它发源于青藏高原，流经青海、四川、西藏、云南、重庆、湖北、湖南、江西、安徽、江苏和上海等11个省、直辖市和自治区，最后在上海流入东海。长江全长6300多公里，是一条名副其实的"长河"。

A song says, "There is a river in the remote east; it is known as the Yangtze River. There is a river in the remote east; it is known as the Yellow River. Although I haven't seen the beautiful Yangtze River, I often swim in it in my dream. Although I haven't heard the grand Yellow River, it often roars and surges in my dream…"

美丽的长江

When you open up a map of China, you'll see the two big rivers like huge dragons — the Yangtze River and the Yellow River on it. Legend says that the two rivers were dragons from heaven. After seeing the severe drought on earth, they transformed themselves into two big rivers to save the people.

The Yangtze River is the biggest river in Asia and also the third biggest river in the world. Originated from Qinghai-Tibet Plateau, it flows through 11 provinces, municipalities and autonomous regions, including Qinghai, Sichuan, Tibet, Yunnan, Chongqing, Hubei, Hunan, Jiangxi, Anhui, Jiangsu and Shanghai, and finally flows into the East Sea. Spanning a length of over 6300 kilometers, as its Chinese name implies, it is a "long river" indeed.

Having the reputation of the "Golden Watercourse", the Yangtze River is the east-west artery of the Chinese water

壮观的黄河

贯穿　guànchuān
to run through

动脉　dòngmài　artery

通航　tōngháng　navigable

货运量　huòyùnliàng
volume quantity of shipment

内河　nèihé　inland river

享有　xiǎngyǒu　to enjoy

流域　liúyù
river basin, valley

密集　mìjí
intensive, concentrated

河段　héduàn
a section of a river

沿岸　yán'àn
along the bank

悠久　yōujiǔ　long

三峡　Sānxiá　three gorges

战场　zhànchǎng　battlefield

李白　Lǐ Bái
Li Bai, a great poet in the Tang Dynasty

诗篇　shīpiān　poems

白帝城　Báidìchéng
Baidi City

名胜古迹　míngshèng gǔjì
historical sites and scenic spots

长江是贯穿中国东西的水上交通大动脉，干流通航里程2800多公里，货运量占全国内河货运量的80%，在中国享有"黄金水道"的美名。

长江流域人口密集，经济发达，成都、重庆、武汉、南京和上海等大城市都在长江沿岸。长江的每个河段都有不同的名字，比方说，江苏省扬州附近的河段叫扬子江，这也是英语里把长江叫作 Yangtze River 的原因。

长江沿岸，历史悠久，风景秀丽。特别是长江三峡，这里曾是三国时期的古战场，曾留下李白等大诗人的诗篇，有白帝城等众多名胜古迹，这里还是世界上最大的水利工程——三峡水电站的所在地。

陕西省西安市的原始人生活遗址

黄河也发源于青藏高原，是中国第二大河，长5400多公里，被誉为中华民族的母亲河。黄河流域历史悠久，气

transportation, with its mainstream navigable waterway spanning over 2,800 kilometers and the volume of shipment taking up 80% of the inland river freight of the whole country.

正在泄洪的长江三峡水电站

Yangtze River Valley has a dense population and developed economy. Big cities like Chengdu, Chongqing, Wuhan, Nanjing and Shanghai, etc. are all located there. Each section of the river is given a name. For example, the section in Yangzhou of Jiangsu Province is called Yangzi River, hence its English name.

The regions along the banks of the Yangtze River boast a long history and beautiful scenery, especially the Three Gorges of the Yangtze River. Here was the ancient battlefield of the Three Kingdoms Period and also the place where some great ancient poets, such as Li Bai, wrote many famous poems. Baidi City and a number of scenic spots and historic sites are found here. It is also the location of the Three Gorges Hydroelectric Power Station, the largest water conservancy project in the world.

三峡大坝建成前长江岸边的白帝城

Also originated from the Qinghai-Tibet Plateau, the Yellow River is the second biggest river in China and spans

黄土高原水土流失很严重

适宜　shìyí　suitable

原始　yuánshǐ　primitive

朝代　cháodài　dynasty

重心　zhòngxīn　center

逐渐　zhújiàn　gradually

转移　zhuǎnyí　to shift

水土流失　shuǐtǔ liúshī
water loss and soil erosion

侧面　cèmiàn
from another aspect

壮观　zhuàngguān
magnificent, splendid

壶口　Húkǒu　Hukou

瀑布　pùbù　waterfall

比喻　bǐyù
to be a metaphor of

战胜　zhànshèng
to overcome

候适宜。早在 110 万年以前，就有原始人在这里生活。从公元前 21 世纪的夏朝到现在，在 4000 多年的历史中，先后有 13 个朝代在黄河流域建立首都，总时间长达 3000 多年。也就是说，在这 3000 年期间，黄河流域一直是中国的政治、经济和文化中心。中国古代的四大发明①都产生于黄河流域。直到北宋以后，全国的经济重心才逐渐由黄河流域向南方长江流域转移。

　　黄河流域水土流失严重，是世界上含沙量最高的河，所以水很浑浊，看上去很黄。有句俗话说"跳进黄河洗不清"②，也侧面反映了这一点。

　　黄河上壮观的壶口瀑布，水流很急，被称为黄河上的"龙门"。传说如果黄河里的鲤鱼跳过"龙门"就会变成龙。现在"鲤鱼跳龙门"常被用来比喻人们战胜了困难，最后取得了成功。

a length of over 5400 kilometers. It is reputed as the "Mother River of the Chinese Nation". The Yellow River Valley is known for its long history and fine climate. As early as 1.1 million years ago, primitive men had already lived here. Starting from the Xia Dynasty of the 21st century BC, in the history of 4000 years, the capitals of 13 dynasties were set up in the Yellow River Valley for over 3000 years, which means it had always been the political, economic and cultural center of China during this long period. The Four Great Inventions of China also made their first appearance here. Not until after the Northern Song Dynasty, did the economic center of the country shift from the Yellow River Valley to the Yangtze River Valley in south China.

Suffering from severe water loss and soil erosion, the Yellow River Valley is the most sediment-laden river on earth, so the water of the river is muddy and yellow. The saying "one is unable to wash oneself clean even if one jumps into the Yellow River" reflects this fact from another aspect.

Known for its torrential current, the splendid Hukou Waterfall of the Yellow River is called the "Dragon Gate". Legend says a carp would become a dragon after it jumps over the "Dragon Gate". Now it is often used to describe one overcomes difficulties and succeeds in the end.

游客们在欣赏壮观的壶口瀑布

文化注释

1 四大发明

中国古代四大发明是指造纸术、印刷术、指南针和火药。

2 跳进黄河洗不清

黄河的水很浑浊，脏东西是洗不干净的。人们常用来说明受到嫌疑和冤枉，跟某件事（一般是不好的事）摆脱不了关系。

◇ 练习 ◇

一 阅读理解 Reading comprehension

练习1：判断正误 Decide whether the following statements are right (√) or wrong (×)

例 长江和黄河两条大河都是自东向西流。(×)

1. 长江和黄河被誉为中华民族的母亲河。(   )

2. 长江是亚洲的第一长河，世界第一长河。(   )

3. 长江流经 11 个省、市和自治区，最后在三峡流入东海。(   )

4. 长江被誉为"黄金水道"，是因为它是贯穿中国东西的水上交通大动脉。
(   )

5. 世界最大的水利工程三峡大坝就建在黄河流域。(   )

6. 早在 110 万年以前，就有原始人在黄河流域生活。(   )

7. 先后有 13 个朝代在黄河流域建立首都，总时间长达 3000 多年。(   )

8. 北宋以后，全国的经济重心逐渐由长江流域转移到黄河流域。(   )

9. 黄河是中国第二大河，是中华民族的"母亲河"。(   )

10. 长江上的壶口瀑布被称为"龙门"。(   )

练习2：选择正确答案 Choose the right answers

例 "谁不曾听见黄河壮，澎湃 ___C___ 在梦里……"

 A. 神游   B. 吸引   C. 汹涌   D. 遥远

1. 长江和黄河的都发源于_____。

 A. 青藏高原   B. 三峡   C. 白帝城   D. 壶口瀑布

2. 传说，天上的两条龙为了_____，化为两条大江大河，留在了人间。

 A. 留在人间   B. 拯救人类 C. 跳过龙门 D. 横卧着

3. 扬子江是指_____附近的河段。

 A. 美丽江南   B. 黄河流域 C. 上海   D. 江苏省扬州

4. 三峡水电站在_____。

 A. 扬子江沿岸 B. 金沙江沿岸 C. 黄河流域 D. 三峡

5. _____是长江沿岸的名胜古迹之一。

 A. 白帝城   B. 壶口瀑布 C. 四大发明 D. 鲤鱼跳龙门

6. 长江流域经济发达，有很多大城市，例如_____等。

 A. 西安、广州 B. 武汉、广州 C. 重庆、武汉 D. 西安、重庆

7. "鲤鱼跳龙门"常用来比喻_____。

 A. 水流很急

 B. 鲤鱼会变成龙

 C. 人们战胜了困难，最后取得了成功

 D. 黄河是母亲河

8. "跳进黄河洗不清"侧面反映了 _____ 。

  A. 黄河水很浑浊   B. 黄河的水很清

  C. 黄河流域气候适宜   D. 黄河流域历史悠久

9. 从夏朝到现在，在 4000 多年的历史中，先后有 13 个朝代在黄河流域

  _____ 。

  A. 发展旅游业   B. 修建水利工程

  C. 建立首都   D. 开辟古战场

10. 中国的"四大发明"都产生于于 _____ 。

  A. 黄河流域   B. 秀美的三峡

  C. 黄金水道   D. 长江上游

▤ 语段练习 Exercises about paragraphs

连线 **Match the statements on the left with those on the right**

1. 遥远的东方有一条河   A. 水上交通大动脉

2. 长江黄河都发源于   B. 都有不同的名字

3. 传说，长江黄河本来是   C. 李白等大诗人的诗篇

4. 长江是贯穿中国东西的   D. 它的名字叫黄河

5. 长江的货运量占   E. 重庆、武汉、南京和上海等

6. 长江的每个河段   F. 就有原始人在黄河流域生活

7. 长江流域的大城市有   G. 是世界上含沙量最高的河

8. 长江三峡曾留下   H. 天上的两条龙

9. 黄河流域水土流失严重   I. 全国内河货运量的 80%

10. 早在 110 万年以前   J. 青藏高原

三 词汇练习 Exercises about vocabulary

用本课所学的新词填空 **Fill in the blanks with the words in this lesson**

发源于	沿岸	货运量	贯穿	流入
流域	本来	原始人	古战场	朝代

　　传说长江和黄河 ___本来___ 是天上的两条龙，这两条大河都 _____ 青藏高原，长江是亚洲的第一长河，流经 11 个省、市和自治区，最后在上海 _____ 东海，全长 6300 多公里。长江被誉为中国的"黄金水道"，因为它是 _____ 中国东西的水上交通大动脉，_____ 占全国内河货运量的 80% 以上。长江 _____ 风景秀丽，历史悠久，还曾是三国时期的 _____ 。黄河是中国第二大河，黄河流域早在 110 万年前，就有 _____ 在黄河流域生活，夏朝之后先后有 13 个 _____ 在黄河流域建立首都，时间长达 3000 多年。在这 3000 多年中，黄河 _____ 一直是中国的政治、经济、文化中心，中国的四大发明也都产生于黄河流域。

四 语法练习 Exercises about grammar

用所给的词语组句 **Make sentences with the words given**

例　全长　长江　6300　公里　多　一条　是　长河　名副其实的
　　<u>长江全长 6300 多公里，是一条名副其实的"长河"。</u>

1. 横卧着的　巨龙一般　所吸引　一定　地图上　两条大河　会被　你

_____

2. 每个　河段　名字　长江的　不同的　都有

_____

3. 有　白帝城　这里　等　名胜古迹　众多

_____

4. 以前　110万年　早在　原始人　就　在　生活　这里　有

_____

5. 黄河流域　和文化中心　3000多年来　政治　中国的　一直是　经济

_____

五 写作练习 Writing practice

用下列词语造句 Make sentences using the following words and phrases

1. 被……所吸引：_____

2. 被誉为……：_____

3. 名副其实：_____

4. 享有……的美名：_____

5. 是……的原因：_____

6. ……的所在地：_____

7. 早在……就……：_____

8. 侧面反映了：_____

9. 被称为：_____

10. ……用来比喻……：_____

西藏那曲的牧场，牦牛正在低头吃草

导读问题　Lead-in questions

1. 你去过雪山吗？
2. 世界上海拔最高的地方在哪儿？
3. 为什么青藏高原上有很多湖，而且还有很多大河的发源地？
4. 青藏高原有什么气候特点？去旅游应注意什么？
5. 青藏高原是怎么形成的？为什么人们都很向往、喜爱青藏高原？

你知道地球上海拔最高的地方是哪里吗？你知道地球上除了寒冷的南极、北极以外，还有同样寒冷的"第三极"吗？

青藏高原风光（青海祁连山）

海拔　hǎibá
altitude, sea level

南极　nánjí
South Pole

北极　běijí
North Pole

青藏高原
Qīng–Zàng Gāoyuán
Qinghai-Tibet Plateau

分布　fēnbù
to be situated

包括　bāokuò
to include

尼泊尔　Níbó'ěr
Nepal

印度　Yìndù
India

屋脊　wūjǐ
roof

覆盖　fùgài
to cover

喜马拉雅山　Xǐmǎlāyǎ Shān
Himalaya

珠穆朗玛峰
Zhūmùlǎngmǎ Fēng
Qomolangma (Mount Everest)

它就是著名的青藏高原。青藏高原主要分布在中国的西南部，包括西藏、青海的全部，四川、新疆、甘肃和云南等地的一部分，除此之外，还有小部分分布在尼泊尔、印度等国家。青藏高原总面积近300万平方公里，其中近250万平方公里位于中国，占中国国土总面积的四分之一左右。

青藏高原平均海拔4000～5000米，因此被称为"世界屋脊"和地球的"第三极"。高原上有很多海拔五六千米以上的大山，这些地方终年被冰雪覆盖。青藏高原南部的喜马拉雅山，是世界上海拔最高的山，它的主峰——珠穆朗玛峰海拔

Do you know the highest place on earth? Do you know besides the cold South Pole, North Pole, there is also the cold "Third Pole"?

It is the famous Qinghai-Tibet Plateau. Qinghai-Tibet Plateau is mostly situated in southwest China, including the entirety of Tibet and Qinghai, part of Sichuan, Xinjiang, Gansu and Yunnan and a small part of Nepal, India and other countries. It has a total land area of nearly 3 million square kilometers, of which nearly 2.5 million square kilometers are in China, taking up approximately one-fourth of China's total land area.

Known as the "Roof of the World" and the "Third Pole" on earth, the Qinghai-Tibet Plateau has an average sea level of 4000-5000 meters. Many mountains on the plateau are more than 5000-6000 meters high and are covered with ice and snow all year round. Located in the south of Qinghai-Tibet Plateau, Himalaya is the highest mountain on earth, with its peak, the

冰雪覆盖的喜马拉雅山

藏语　Zàngyǔ
Tibetan (language)

女神　nǚshén
goddess

雅鲁藏布江
Yǎlǔzàngbù Jiāng
Yarlung Tsangpo River

冰川　bīngchuān
glacier

融水　róngshuǐ
meltwater

竟然　jìngrán
even (unexpectedly)

挡住　dǎngzhù
to block, to stop

暖湿　nuǎnshī
warm and moist

干燥　gānzào　dry

稀薄　xībó　thin

氧气　yǎngqì
oxygen

剧烈　jùliè　strenuous

防晒　fángshài
sun block

渴望　kěwàng
desire; to yearn for

半路　bànlù
halfway

长眠　chángmián
to die, to sleep forever

8844.43 米，是世界上最高的山峰。在藏语中，"喜马拉雅"是"冰雪之乡"的意思，"珠穆朗玛"是"大地之母"、"女神"的意思。

高山上冰雪非常多，融化之后汇聚成了很多湖和河流。位于青海省的青海湖面积为 4456 平方公里，是中国最大的湖。长江、黄河、印度河和雅鲁藏布江等都发源于青藏高原，其中雅鲁藏布江是世界上海拔最高的河，被称为"天河"。点点滴滴的冰川融水，最后竟然汇成了一条条奔腾的大江大河，不禁让人感叹自然的神奇。

青藏高原非常高，不但挡住了来自北方大陆的冷空气，使得冷空气进入不了南亚，也挡住了来自南亚的暖湿空气——所以南亚总是那么热，那么多雨，而喜马拉雅山的北面却又寒冷又干燥。

青藏高原因为海拔高，所以空气很稀薄，阳光照射比较强。去那儿旅游的人，因为氧气不足，不能做剧烈的运动，还要注意防晒。珠穆朗玛峰永远是很多登山运动员最渴望的目标，有一些运动员最后登上了珠穆朗玛峰，也有许多人倒在了半路上，长眠在世界屋脊。

8,844.43-meter-high Mount Qomolangma (Mount Everest) being the highest peak in the world. In Tibetan, Himalaya means "the land of ice and snow" and Qomolangma means "mother of the earth" or "goddess".

The mountain is covered with thick ice and snow. After they are melted, they become many lakes and rivers. Being the biggest lake of China, Qinghai Lake with an area of 4456 square kilometers is located in Qinghai Province. All the Yangtze River, the Yellow River, the Indian River and the Yarlung Tsangpo River are originated from Qinghai-Tibet Plateau. Among them, the Yarlung Tsangpo River, known as the "Heavenly River", is the river with the highest sea level in the world. The meltwater from the glacier is accumulated and converged into big torrential rivers. How wonderful is the Mother Nature!

The high Qinghai-Tibet Plateau not only blocks the cold air from the

雅鲁藏布汇大峡谷

northern continent, making it impossible for the cold air to enter south Asia, it also stops the warm and moist air from south Asia. That explains why south Asia is always so hot and rainy and the north of Himalaya is always so

可可西里自然保护区内的野驴群

珍稀 zhēnxī
rare

濒危 bīnwēi
endangered

地质 dìzhì
geology

地貌 dìmào
landform

独特 dútè
unique

本底 běndǐ
background

神话 shénhuà
myth

起初 qǐchū
at first

亿 yì
a hundred million

板块 bǎnkuài
plate

形成 xíngchéng
to form; formation

　　青藏高原设有形形色色的各类自然保护区，有珍稀濒危动物自然保护区，植物自然保护区、还有地质地貌自然保护区，等等。在全球最高、自然环境最为独特、多样的区域内建立各类保护区，不仅为人类提供了高原自然界的原始"本底"，保护了许多珍稀濒危动植物，而且也为开展有关青藏高原的地学、生物学等学科的研究，提供了理想的基地和天然实验室。

　　中国有一个"沧海桑田"的神话，传说天上有一个女神，她看到人世间有好几次大海变成了农田，农田又变成了大海。起初人们觉得这不可能，而现在科学已经证明，20亿年前的青藏高原，就曾经是大海，后来由于地球的板块运动，陆地慢慢升起，才形成了今天的青

cold and dry.

The air is thin and the sunshine is strong on Qinghai-Tibet Plateau because of its high sea level. Since oxygen is deficient, travelers cannot do strenuous exercises or be exposed to direct sunshine. For many mountaineers, climbing Qomolangma has always been what they want to do the most. Some of them reached the top of the Mount Everest at last, while many others died on their way to it, and slept on the Roof of the World forever.

Qinghai-Tibet Plateau has a variety of natural reserves for rare and endangered animals, plants, geology and geomorphology, etc. The establishment of such reserves on the highest place on earth with the most unique and diverse natural environment not only provides the primitive "background" of the plateau for human beings, protects many rare and endangered animals and plants, but also provides an ideal base and natural laboratory for the research in disciplines like geology and biology of Qinghai-Tibet Plateau.

There is a Chinese myth about the transformation of the world. It says a goddess witnessed the sea had changed into farmland and the farmland into sea several times. At first, people feel it was impossible, but now science has proved

珠穆朗玛峰

向往　　xiàngwǎng
to yearn for

藏高原。大约一万年前，地球的板块运动加快，珠穆朗玛峰平均每100年上升7米，现在还在慢慢长呢！如果你10年后去为珠穆朗玛峰量一量"身高"，它肯定又长高了。

在中国，甚至世界上，有很多人都很向往青藏高原，有一首叫作《青藏高原》的歌曲表达了人们对它的喜爱："……我看见一座座山，一座座山川，一座座山川相连，那就是青藏高原……"

如今，架设在高原上的青藏铁路①已经开通了，如果坐火车去西藏，非常方便，一路上还可以看到高耸的山峰、清澈的湖水，甚至奔跑的藏羚羊。

西藏昌都地区的然乌湖，由高山冰川融化汇集而成

世界上海拔最高的铁路——青藏铁路

that Qinghai-Tibet Plateau was a sea 2 billion years ago. With the plate movement, the land gradually rose and today's Qinghai-Tibet Plateau came into existence. About 10 thousand years ago, the earth accelerated its plate movement, and Qomolangma rose 7 meters every 100 years. Now it is still growing taller. If you measure its height after ten years, you'll surely find it will be taller.

Many people in China and in other countries look forward to going to Qinghai-Tibet Plateau. A song known as *Qinghai-Tibet Plateau* expresses people's fondness for it, "…I see so many mountains; One by one, connected to each other. This is Qinghai-Tibet Plateau…"

Nowadays, Qinghai-Tibet Railway on the Plateau is open. It is very comvenient for you to go to Tibet by train, and you'll see on your way the towering peaks, clear lake water and even the running Tibetan antelopes.

文化注释

❶ 青藏铁路

　　为了促进西部的开发，中国修建了青藏铁路。青藏铁路从青海西宁开始，一直到西藏的拉萨，是世界上海拔最高、线路最长的高原铁路，被人们叫作"天路"。青藏铁路开通后，从北京坐火车到拉萨只需要 48 个小时。

◇ 练习 ◇

阅读理解 Reading comprehension

练习 1：判断正误 Decide whether the following statements are right（√）or wrong（×）

例　青藏高原的喜马拉雅山是世界上最高的山。（ √ ）

1. 青藏高原主要分布在中国的西北部。（　　）

2. 珠穆朗玛峰是喜马拉雅山的主峰，海拔 8844.43 米。（　　）

3. 喜马拉雅山位于青藏高原的西部，是世界上海拔最高的山。（　　）

4. 青藏高原平均海拔 4000 ～ 5000 米，因此被称为"世界屋脊"。（　　）

5. "喜马拉雅"在藏语中的意思是"大地之母"。（　　）

6. 亚洲许多大河都发源于青藏高原，例如长江、黄河、印度河和雅鲁藏布江等。（　　）

7. 雅鲁藏布江位于青藏高原的东部，是世界上海拔最高的河。（　　）

8. 雅鲁藏布江被称为"天河"是因为它的江水像天空一样蓝。（　　）

9. 青藏高原挡住了来自北方大陆的冷空气，所以高原以南很少下雨。（　　）

10. 青藏高原的海拔太高了，所以氧气不足，阳光照射强。（　　）

例 中国著名的青藏高原被称为 ___B___ 。

    A. 冰雪之乡　　　　B. 世界屋脊　　　　C. 大地之母　　　　D. 女神

1. 青藏高原因为缺氧，所以不能 _____ 。

    A. 找到很多湖　　B. 被冰雪覆盖　　C. 做剧烈运动　　D. 种植物

2. 雅鲁藏布江是世界上_____的河流。

    A. 海拔最高　　　B. 最长　　　　C. 最寒冷　　　　D. 最北部

3. "喜马拉雅"在藏语中的意思是_____。

    A. 发源地　　　　B. 冰川融水　　C. 大地之母　　　D. 冰雪之乡

4. 青藏高原挡住了_____，所以喜马拉雅山的北面又寒冷又干燥。

    A. 点点滴滴的冰川融水　　　　　　B. 来自南亚的暖湿空气

    C. 稀薄的空气　　　　　　　　　　D. 地球的板块运动

5. 现在科学已经证明20亿年前的青藏高原，曾经是_____。

    A. 陆地　　　　　B. 农田　　　　C. 大海　　　　　D. 冰川

6. 青藏高原的总面积近300万平方公里，主要分布在中国的_____。

    A. 云南　　　　　B. 四川　　　　C. 东北部　　　　D. 西南部

7. 由于地球的板块运动加快，陆地_____，才形成了青藏高原。

    A. 又寒冷又多雨　　　　　　　　　B. 慢慢升起

    C. 被冰雪覆盖　　　　　　　　　　D. 出现很多湖泊

8. 青藏高原也是_____许多大河的发源地。

    A. 亚洲　　　　　B. 非洲　　　　C. 欧洲　　　　　D. 世界

9. 喜马拉雅山是世界上最高的山，位于青藏高原的 _____。

    A. 南部   B. 中部   C. 北部   D. 西北部

10. 雅鲁藏布江所以被称为"天河"，是因为 _____。

    A. 它挡住了北方的冷空气   B. 平均每 100 年上升 7 米

    C. 它是世界上海拔最高的河   D. 终年被冰雪覆盖

二 语段练习 Exercises about paragraphs

连线 **Match the statements on the left with those on the right**

1. 世界上最高的山峰是	A. 地球的"第三极"
2. 青藏高原主要分布在	B. 4000 ~ 5000 米
3. 著名的青藏高原被称为	C. 青藏高原
4. 青藏高原的平均海拔是	D. 珠穆朗玛峰
5. 青藏高原的山脉终年	E. 最渴望的目标
6. 许多大河的发源地都是	F. 非常寒冷，而且很干燥
7. 喜马拉雅山的北部	G. 中国的西藏、青海一带
8. 在青藏高原旅游	H. 曾经是大海
9. 珠穆朗玛峰永远是很多登山运动员	I. 不能做剧烈的运动
10. 20 亿年前的青藏高原	J. 被冰雪覆盖

三 词汇练习 Exercises about vocabulary

用本课所学的新词填空 **Fill in the blanks with the words in this lesson**

海拔	融化	剧烈	终年	发源于
干燥	渴望	主峰	分布	多种多样

　　青藏高原主要　_分布_　在中国的西南部，平均海拔 4000 米 ~ 5000 米，因此被称为"世界屋脊"和地球的"第三极"。青藏高原有三高：世界上＿＿＿＿最高的山——喜马拉雅山，世界上海拔最高的山峰——珠穆朗玛峰，世界上海拔最高的河流——雅鲁藏布江。青藏高原的高山＿＿＿＿被冰雪覆盖。珠穆朗玛峰海拔 8844.43 米，由于地球的板块运动，珠穆朗玛峰平均每 100 年上升 7 米，它是喜马拉雅山的＿＿＿＿，是世界上最高的山峰，也是很多登山运动员最＿＿＿＿的目标。高山上冰雪非常多，＿＿＿＿之后汇聚成了很多湖和河流。青海省的青海湖，是中国最大的湖。长江、黄河、印度河和雅鲁藏布江等都＿＿＿＿这里。雅鲁藏布江是世界上海拔最高的河，被称为"天河"。 青藏高原非常高，喜马拉雅山的北面寒冷又＿＿＿＿。空气很稀薄，阳光照射比较强。去那儿旅游的人，因为氧气不足，不能做＿＿＿＿的运动，还要注意防晒。青藏高原设有＿＿＿＿的自然保护区，为开展研究，提供了理想的基地和天然实验室。

四 语法练习 Exercises about grammar

用所给的词语组句 **Make sentences with the words given**

例　西南部　青藏高原　中国的　分布　主要　在
　　青藏高原主要分布在中国的西南部。

1. 大河的　发源地　是　亚洲　许多　青藏高原

_____

2. 因为　所以　"天河"　雅鲁藏布江　河　世界上　是　海拔最高的　被称为

_____

3. 冷空气　来自　挡住了　青藏高原　北方大陆的

_____

_____

4. 登山运动员　目标　永远是　很多　最渴望的　珠穆朗玛峰

_____

_____

5. 平均　珠穆朗玛峰　100 年　每　7 米　上升

_____

_____

五 写作练习 Writing practice

用下列词语造句 Make sentences using the following words and phrases

1. 除了……以外，还…… : _____

2. 除此之外 : _____

3. 被称为 : _____

4. 终年 : _____

5. 不禁 : _____

6. 不但……也…… : _____

7. 形形色色 : _____

8. 不仅……而且…… : _____

9. 由于……才 : _____

10. 甚至 : _____

内蒙古大草原

草原上正在吃草的羊群

导读问题　Lead-in questions

1. 你去过草原吗？去过哪个草原？
2. 草原上雪白的"小帐篷"是什么？它们有什么用？
3. 关于马头琴有什么故事？
4. 那达慕大会是什么节日？你想去那里看看吗？
5. 你对内蒙古大草原总的印象（impression）是什么？

飘	piāo	to float
挥	huī	to wave
鞭	biān	to whip
飞翔	fēixiáng	to fly

内蒙古　Nèiměnggǔ
Inner Mongolia

草原　cǎoyuán
grassland

迷人　mírén
charming, fascinating

天然　tiānrán　**natural**

一望无际　yíwàng wújì
to stretch as far as the eye can see

成群　chéngqún
in groups / flocks

欢快　huānkuài　cheerful

地毯　dìtǎn　carpet

点缀　diǎnzhuì
to embellish, to intersperse

清香　qīngxiāng　fragrant

清新　qīngxīn　fresh

湛蓝　zhànlán　azure

飘逸　piāoyì　floating

美妙　měimiào　wonderful

令人神往
lìngrén shénwǎng
to take one's breath away, to be fascinating

散布　sànbù　to scatter

"蓝蓝的天上白云飘，白云下面马儿跑。挥动鞭儿响四方，百鸟齐飞翔。"如果你想知道在哪里能看到这像画儿一样的美景，那么你一定要去中国内蒙古大草原，去感受那儿的迷人景色。

白云下在吃草的羊群

内蒙古大草原是中国面积最大的草原，占全中国天然草原总面积的四分之一。草原上一望无际，到处都能看见成群的牛、羊、马，听见它们欢快的叫声。大草原就像一块儿绿色的大地毯，上面点缀着五颜六色的鲜花。牛群羊群在绿色的地毯中走动，一阵风吹过，清香阵阵。清新的空气，湛蓝的天空，飘逸的白云，奔跑的牛羊……如此美妙的大自然，真是令人神往。

在这一望无际的大草原上，还散布着很多雪白的"小帐篷"，它们有的

"The white clouds are floating in the blue sky, under which horses are running happily. The sound of the horsewhip travels far in all directions, and hundreds of birds are flying and dancing in the sky..." If you want to see this picturesque scenery, please come to the grassland of the Inner Mongolia of China.

The grassland of the Inner Mongolia of China is the largest grassland in China, taking up a quarter of the total grassland area of the country. On the endless grassland, one can see flocks of cattle, sheep and horses, and hear their happy neighs, moos and baas. The grassland is like a large green carpet, which is dotted with flowers of various colors. Herds of cows and sheep are walking on this green carpet, with fragrance in the breeze. The clean air, blue sky, floating white clouds and galloping cows and sheep...the wonderful Mother Nature will take your breath away.

呼伦贝尔草原上奔跑的马群

挨　āi
to be close to

蒙古包　měnggǔbāo
(Mongolian) yurt

牧民　mùmín
herdsman, shepherd

游牧　yóumù
nomad

搬迁　bānqiān
to move

传出　chuánchū
to come out

悠扬　yōuyáng
melodious

马头琴　mǎtóuqín
horse-head *qin*

动人　dòngrén
touching

牧童　mùtóng
cowboy

形影不离　xíngyǐng bùlí
inseparable

王爷　wángye
Royal Highness

赛　sài
race

冠军　guànjūn
champion

草原上的蒙古包

挨在一起，有的分开，好像一座座小雪山——它们就是蒙古包，草原上的牧民就住在这里。牧民们因为长期过着游牧生活，不断迁移，而蒙古包容易建造和搬迁，所以非常适合牧民们居住。蒙古包里经常会传出悠扬的马头琴声，非常动听。

　　马头琴是蒙古人非常喜欢的一种乐器。关于马头琴，有一个很动人的传说：很久以前，有一个蒙古族牧童叫苏和，他在回家的路上捡到了一匹小白马，便将它带回了家中。在他的照顾下，小白马一天天地长大了，它浑身雪白，美丽健壮，每天与苏和形影不离。一年春天，草原上的王爷举行了一次赛马大会，苏和骑着自己心爱的小白马，参加比赛获得了冠军。可比赛后，王爷却抢走了苏和的小白马。小白马为了回

Many white small tents are also scattered on the endless grassland, some of which are built side by side, while others are separated, looking like little snowy hills. Known as yurts, they are herdsmen's residences. Since herdsmen have always been constantly on the move and a yurt is easy to build and move, it is very suitable for herdsmen's nomadic life. One can often hear the melodious and thouching music played with horse-head *qin* (a kind of stringed musical instrument) coming out of the yurts.

Horse-head *qin* is a kind of musical instrument that Mongolians love. There is a touching story about it. Long ago, there was a Mongolian cowboy named Su He who found a little white pony on his way and brought it back home. Under his care, the little pony grew up as time wore on. It was snow-white, beautiful and strong and always followed Su He wherever he went. One spring, the Royal Highness had a horse race on the grassland. Riding

草原上的赛马活动

逃跑　táopǎo
to escape

箭　jiàn
arrow

射　shè
to shoot

茶饭不思　cháfàn bùsī
to have no appetite

梦见　mèngjiàn
to dream

筋骨　jīngǔ
sinews and bones

醒来　xǐnglái
to wake up

模样　múyàng
appearance

雕刻　diāokè
to carve

传遍　chuánbiàn
to spread across

袍　páo　robe, gown

小伙子　xiǎohuǒzi
lad, young man

靴　xuē　boots

潇洒　xiāosǎ
natural and unrestrained

到苏和身边，逃跑了好几次，后来被王爷用箭射死了。苏和知道后非常难过，好几天茶饭不思。一天夜里，苏和梦见了小白马，它告诉苏和："你如果想让我永远跟你在一起，那就用我身上的筋骨做一只琴吧！"苏和醒来以后，就按照小白马的话，用它的筋骨做成了一只琴，最后在琴顶部照着小白马的模样雕刻了一个马头。每当苏和

马头琴

想念小白马的时候，便会拉起这个琴。人们听到后很喜欢这种琴的声音，后来，马头琴就传遍了整个草原。当然，现在的马头琴不是用马的筋骨做成的，而是用木头等材料做的。

　　草原牧民穿的服装也很特别，叫作蒙古袍。为了方便骑马，蒙古族人都穿自制的蒙古靴子。年轻的小伙子穿上蒙古袍和马靴，看上去非常英俊、潇洒；

his beloved little white horse, Su He entered the race and took the crown. But after the race, the Royal Highness snatched the horse. To go back to Su He, the little white horse tried to escape several times and finally was shot by the Royal Highness. Su He was very sad at the news and had

蒙古族服饰

no appetite for several days. One night, Su He met the little white horse in his dream. It told him, "If you want me to be always with you, make a *qin* out of my sinews and bones." After Su He woke up, he made a *qin* using the horse's sinews and bones and carved a horse's head on top of the *qin* exactly like his little white horse's. Whenever he missed the little white horse, he

would play the *qin*. People liked to hear the *qin* very much, and later horse-head *qin* became popular across the grassland. Of course, the *qin* is now made of wood and other materials, not a horse's sinews and bones.

那达慕大会开幕式

苗条　miáotiao　slender

北纬　běiwěi
north latitude

擅长　shàncháng
to be good at

奶产品　nǎichǎnpǐn
dairy product

奶茶　nǎichá
milk tea

奶豆腐　nǎidòufu
milk tofu

好客　hàokè
hospitable

招待　zhāodài
to entertaina (a guest)

热闹　rènao
lively, bustling

摔跤　shuāi jiāo
wrestling

女孩子穿上蒙古袍，看起来很漂亮、很苗条。

据说北纬 40 ~ 45 度之间的地方非常适合养奶牛，生产牛奶，而内蒙古大草原正好就位于北纬 40 ~ 45 度之间。草原上的人们擅长制作各种奶产品，比如奶茶、奶酒和奶豆腐。热情好客的蒙古族人常常用他们的奶茶、奶酒招待客人。

要是问什么时候去草原最好，那一定是在阳历 7 月和 8 月的时候。这时候，草原上不但风景漂亮，而且还是草原上最热闹的日子，因为这时正值蒙古族人们庆祝他们自己的节日——那达慕大会①。那达慕大会可以说是内蒙古大草原上的牧民们最重要的节日，人们可以买卖东西，还会举办骑马、射箭、摔跤等比赛，非常热闹！

草原上的奶牛

Herdsmen on the grassland wear a special costume, which is known as the Mongolian robe. For the convenience of riding horses, they all wear self-made boots. Young lads look handsome

那达慕大会上的摔跤手

and carefree in Mongolian robes and boots, while girls wearing Mongolian robes look beautiful and slender.

People on the grassland are good at making various diary products, for example, milk tea, milk wine and milk tofu. Hospitable Mongolians often entertain their guests with milk tea and milk wine. It is said that cows grow best in places with a latitude between 40-45 degrees north, which is exactly the location of the Inner Mongolia Grassland.

July and August are surely the best time to visit the grassland. It is not only beautiful, but also bustling because Mongolians celebrate their own festival—Naadam during this time. Naadam is the most important festival for herdsmen on the grassland of the Inner Mongolia, when people do shopping, have contests of horse-riding, archery and wrestling and other activities.

文化注释

① 那达慕大会

"那达慕"是蒙古语，"慕"是蒙古语"娱乐、游戏"的意思。那达慕大会是蒙古族人民喜爱的一种传统体育活动形式，也是蒙古族人民一年一度的传统盛会，每年农历六月初四（多在草绿花红、羊肥马壮的阳历 7 月或 8 月）开始。

◇ 练习 ◇

一 阅读理解 Reading comprehension

练习 1：判断正误 Decide whether the following statements are right (√) or wrong (×)

例 内蒙古大草原是中国面积最大的草原，占全中国天然草原的十分之一。(×)

1. 在一望无际的大草原上，雪白的蒙古包都挨在一起。(　　)

2. 蒙古包像一座座小雪山，所以非常适合牧民们的居住。(　　)

3. 马头琴是蒙古族人民非常喜欢的一种乐器。(　　)

4. 很久以前，苏和从"那达慕"大会上买回了一匹小白马。(　　)

5. 苏和在琴顶部照着小白马的模样雕刻了一个马头。(　　)

6. 蒙古族人都穿自制的蒙古靴子，是为了方便走路。(　　)

7. 奶茶、奶酒是蒙古族人民从外地买来招待客人用的。(　　)

8. 内蒙古大草原主要位于北纬 50 ～ 60 度之间。(　　)

9. 那达慕大会是内蒙古大草原上的牧民们最重要的节日。(　　)

10. 那达慕大会有各种活动，例如骑马比赛、射箭比赛等。(　　)

练习 2：选择正确答案 Choose the right answers

例 内蒙古大草原是 _____B_____ 面积最大的草原。

A. 世界　　　　　　B. 中国　　　　　　C. 亚洲　　　　　　D. 中国北部

1. 在大草原上，_____ 能看见成群的牛、羊、马，听见它们欢快的叫声。

A. 到处都　　　　　B. 星星点点　　　　C. 偶尔　　　　　　D. 好几天

2. 内蒙古草原一望无际，就像一块儿绿色的大地毯。"一望无际"的意思是

_____。

A. 看不到边际　　　B. 清楚可见　　　　C. 看不见　　　　　D. 平平坦坦

3. _____ 的蒙古包，有的挨在一起，有的分开，好像一座座小山。

A. 雪白　　　　　　B. 五颜六色　　　　C. 绿色　　　　　　D. 黑色

4. 小白马浑身雪白，美丽健壮，每天与苏和 _____。

A. 热情好客　　　　B. 动荡起伏　　　　C. 令人神往　　　　D. 形影不离

5. 王爷用箭射死了小白马，苏和悲痛万分，好几天 _____。

A. 形影不离　　　　B. 茶饭不思　　　　C. 不骑马　　　　　D. 不睡觉

6. 为了 _____，蒙古族人都穿自制的蒙古靴子。

A. 看上去英俊　　　　　　　　　　B. 方便骑马

C. 参加骑马比赛　　　　　　　　　D. 听见悠扬的马头琴声

7. 热情好客的蒙古族人们常常用他们制作的 _____ 招待客人。

A. 五颜六色的鲜花　　　　　　　　B. 蒙古靴子

C. 马头琴声　　　　　　　　　　　D. 奶茶、奶酒

113

8. 草原上的人们_____ 制作各种奶产品。

   A. 雕刻　　　　　　B. 擅长　　　　　　C. 潇洒　　　　　　D. 苗条

9. 每年的_____ 会在草原上举行"那达慕"大会。

   A. 七八月　　　　　B. 十月　　　　　　C. 四月　　　　　　D. 冬天

10. 在那达慕大会上，人们可以买卖东西，还会举办骑马、射箭、_____ 等
    比赛。

   A. 跑步　　　　　　B. 滑冰　　　　　　C. 游泳　　　　　　D. 摔跤

语段练习 Exercises about paragraphs

连线 **Match the statements on the left with those on the right**

1. 内蒙古大草原的面积占　　　　　A. 形影不离

2. 大草原就像一块儿大地毯　　　　B. 游牧生活，不断迁移

3. 草原上的牧民长期过着　　　　　C. 用它的筋骨做了一只琴

4. 小白马每天跟苏和　　　　　　　D. 全中国天然草原总面积的四分之一

5. 苏和骑着小白马　　　　　　　　E. 便会拉起这个马头琴

6. 小白马死后，苏和非常难过　　　F. 上面点缀着五颜六色的鲜花

7. 苏和按照小白马的话　　　　　　G. 参加赛马大会，获得了冠军

8. 每当苏和想他的小白马时　　　　H. 好几天茶饭不思

9. 草原牧民穿的服装　　　　　　　I. 风景漂亮，而且还是最热闹的日子

10. 七八月的时候，草原上不但　　　J. 叫作蒙古袍

三 词汇练习 Exercises about vocabulary

用本课所学的新词填空 Fill in the blanks with the words in this lesson

招待	蒙古包	一望无际	摔跤	欢快
奶产品	游牧	乐器	占	传出

　　内蒙古大草原是中国面积最大的草原，＿占＿全中国天然草原总面积的四分之一。草原上＿＿＿＿＿，到处都能看见成群的牛、羊、马，听见它们＿＿＿＿＿的叫声。在大草原上，还可以看到很多雪白的＿＿＿＿＿。草原上的牧民就住在这些蒙古包里，因为他们长期过着＿＿＿＿＿生活，蒙古包非常适合他们居住。草原牧民穿的服装也很特别，叫蒙古袍。为了方便骑马，蒙古族人都穿自制的蒙古靴子。马头琴是蒙古族人民非常喜欢的一种＿＿＿＿＿，蒙古包里常常会＿＿＿＿＿悠扬的马头琴声。草原上的人民制作出很多＿＿＿＿＿，比如说奶茶、奶酒和奶豆腐。热情好客的蒙古族人民常常用他们的奶茶、奶酒＿＿＿＿＿客人。每年七八月举行的那达慕大会是生活在内蒙古大草原上的牧民们最重要的节日。在那达慕大会上，人们可以买卖东西，还举办骑马、射箭、＿＿＿＿＿等比赛。

四 语法练习 Exercises about grammar

用所给的词语组句 Make sentences with the words given

例　面积　是　最大的　中国　内蒙古大草原　草原
　　<u>内蒙古大草原是中国面积最大的草原。</u>

1. 绿色的　内蒙古草原　一块儿　就像　一望无际　大地毯

_____

2. 蒙古包　建造　和　容易　搬迁　非常　所以　牧民们　适合　居住

_____

3. 每当　的时候　小白马　苏和　便会　想起　这个琴　拉起

_____

4. 马靴　年轻的　看上去　穿上　潇洒　蒙古袍　和　小伙子　非常　英俊

_____

5. 那达慕大会　节日　是　牧民们　内蒙古　大草原上的　最重要的

_____

五 写作练习 Writing practice

用下列词语造句　Make sentences using the following words and phrases

1. 如果……那么……：_____

2. 一望无际：_____

3. ……就像……：_____

4. 令人神往：_____

5. 悠扬动听：_____

6. 形影不离：_____

7. 茶饭不思：_____

8. 每当……的时候：_____

9. 传遍了：_____

10. 看上去：_____

上有天堂，下有苏杭

苏州拙政园的长廊

1. 你去过苏州吗？
2. "上有天堂，下有苏杭"是什么意思？
3. 中国的"四大名园"分别是什么？它们有什么不同？
4. 杭州西湖一年四季的美景都是什么？
5. 如果让你选择，你喜欢住在苏州还是杭州？为什么？

天堂　tiāntáng
heaven, paradise

凡是　fánshì
all, any, every

称赞　chēngzàn
to praise

园林　yuánlín
garden

吸引　xīyǐn
to attract

公元前　gōngyuán qián
BC (Before Christ)

繁华　fánhuá
prosperous, flourishing

私家　sījiā
private

游客　yóukè
tourist

无论　wúlùn
no matter what / which /
where / how, etc.

完美　wánměi
perfect

亭台楼阁　tíngtái lóugé
a pavilion, terrace or a tower

中国有一句话："上有天堂，下有苏杭。"这里的"苏杭"是指中国的苏州和杭州这两个地方，意思是说，苏州和杭州非常美，就像天堂一样。

确实，凡是去过苏州、杭州的人，没有一个不称赞苏州那一个个大大小小、各具特色的园林，也没有一个不被杭州那风景如画的西湖所吸引。

江苏苏州的网狮园

苏州位于江苏省的南部，离中国最大的城市上海很近。苏州城最早建于公元前514年，至今已有2500多年的历史。明清时期，苏州是中国最繁华的地区之一，有许多大大小小的私家花园（现在被叫作园林），最多的时候有500多个，现在保存完好的有十几处。苏州园林各具特色，但是它们都有一个共同的特点：游客无论站在哪个点上，眼前总是一幅完美的图画；无论是亭台楼阁、

There is a Chinese saying, "Up above there is Heaven, and down below there are Suzhou and Hangzhou", which indicates the two Chinese cities are as beautiful as heaven.

苏州狮子林的亭台楼阁

It is quite right. No matter who visits Suzhou and Hangzhou, he will praise the various types of gardens of Suzhou and be fascinated by the picturesque West Lake of Hangzhou.

Built in 514 BC with a history of over 2500 years, Suzhou is located in south Jiangsu Province close to Shanghai. It was one of the most prosperous areas of China during the Ming and Qing dynasties, with the number of private gardens (now known as gardens) in it up to over 500, and more than ten of them being best preserved now. Although all the gardens of Suzhou are distinctive, they have one characteristic in common: wherever a visitor goes, he sees a perfect picture. No matter there is a pavilion,

苏州留园的荷花

119

假山　jiǎshān
rockery

池塘　chítáng
pond

游廊　yóuláng
veranda, covered corridor

拙政园　Zhuōzhèng Yuán
Humble Administrator's
Garden

承德　Chéngdé
Chengde, a city of Hebei
Province

避暑山庄　Bìshǔ Shānzhuāng
Mountain Summer Resort

皇家　huángjiā
royal

规模　guīmó
scale

建筑　jiànzhù
architecture

典型　diǎnxíng
typical

颐和园　Yíhé Yuán
the Summer Palace

小吃　xiǎochī　snack
刺绣　cìxiù
embroidery

假山池塘，还是游廊门窗、花草树木，都让游览者能产生"如在图画中"的感觉。

承德避暑山庄风景

苏州最有名的园林是建于明代的拙政园和建于清代的留园。虽然这两个私家园林与北京的颐和园和承德的避暑山庄等皇家园林相比，规模要小得多，但因为它们是中国南方地区民间建筑的典型代表，所以拙政园、留园与北京的颐和园、承德的避暑山庄一起被称为中国的"四大名园"。

著名的寒山寺也位于苏州，近年，有很多国外的游客，特别是日本、韩国的游客，专程在元旦、除夕的时候，到寒山寺听新年钟声，非常有意思。

苏州的小吃品种非常丰富，蜜汁豆腐干、松子糖……你一定要尝一尝。刺绣、

a terrace, or a tower, a rockery or a pond, a covered corrndor, a gate or a window, flowers, grass or trees; every landscape makes one have the feeling of walking in a picture.

苏州寒山寺

The Humble Administrator's Garden built in the Ming Dynasty and the Lingering Garden built in the Qing Dynasty are the most famous gardens in Suzhou. Though much smaller than the Summer Palace of Beijing and the Mountain Summer Resort of Chengde, they are typical examples of the folk architecture in south China. So, the Humble Administrator's Garden and the Lingering Garden, together with the Summer Palace of Beijing and the Mountain Summer Resort of Chengde, are reputed as the "Four Great Gardens of China".

The famous Hanshan Temple is also located in Suzhou. In recent years, many foreign tourists, especially those from Japan and Korea, delieberately went there to listen to the ringing of the bell to announce the New Year on the first day of the first Gregorian month or on New Year's Eve.

Suzhou's snacks are rich in variety, including honey tofu, pine-nut candy, etc.

刺绣绣制的猫

扇　shàn　fan

收藏　shōucáng
to collect

省会　shěnghuì
provincial capital

马可·波罗　Mǎkě·Bōluó
Marco Polo, a famous Italian
traveler of the 13th century

华贵　huáguì　luxurious

景点　jǐngdiǎn
scenic destination, scenic
spot

环　huán
ring; surrounded

风景　fēngjǐng　scenery

四季　sìjì　four seasons

荷花　héhuā　lotus

西施　Xīshī
Xish, name of one of the
most beautiful women in
ancient China

浓妆淡抹　nóngzhuāng dànmǒ
either with light or heavy
makeup

相宜　xiāngyí　appropriate

雷峰塔　Léifēng Tǎ
Leifeng Pogoda

《白蛇传》　Báishé Zhuàn
*The Legend of the White
Snake*

岳飞庙　Yuè Fēi Miào
Yue Fei Temple

纸扇、玉石等手工艺品也是苏州的特产，值得收藏。

杭州是浙江省的省会。杭州的历史也很长，有 2200 多年。它还曾经是南宋时期的首都，是中国的六大古都之一，被马可·波罗称为"世界上最美丽华贵之城"。

春天的杭州西湖

杭州最有名的景点是西湖。西湖在杭州市内，三面环山，风景非常美丽。西湖一年四季各有不同的美景：春天，是西湖边的绿柳红花；夏天，是湖中的荷花；秋天是空中那大又亮的月亮；冬天，则是西湖的白雪。有人把西湖比作古代的美女西施，说"若把西湖比西子，淡妆浓抹总相宜"。意思是西湖就像一个美女，不管怎么打扮，都非常漂亮。

西湖边上的雷峰塔，因为《白蛇传》①的故事而让人好奇；附近的岳飞庙，

You are strongly suggested to have a try. Suzhou also has specialties such as embroidery, paper fans, jade and other handicrafts, all of which are worth collecting.

夏天的杭州西湖

With a history of over 2200 years, Hangzhou is the capital of Zhejiang Province. Being the capital of the Southern Song Dynasty, it was one of the six ancient capitals of China and was reputed by Marco Polo as the "most beautiful and luxurious city in the world".

The West Lake is the most famous scenic spot in Hangzhou. Sitting in the city and surrounded by mountains on three sides, it is very beautiful in different ways during the four seasons. It is famous for the green willows and red flowers along the Lake in spring, the lotus in summer, the big and bright moon in the autumn sky and the white snow on the Lake in winter.

In a poem, the Lake is likened to Xishi, a beauty of ancient China: "The West Lake is like the fair lady at her best, who always looks gorgeous whether she is richly adorned or plainly dressed".

Leifeng Pagoda along the bank of the West Lake arouses people's curiosity for the legend of the White Snake, while the adjacent Yue Fei Temple adds much historical flavor to the Lake.

冬日的杭州西湖

增添　zēngtiān
to add

气息　qìxī
breath, flavor

运河　yùnhé
canal

钱塘江大潮

Qiántáng Jiāng Dàcháo
Qiantang Tide

喇叭　lǎba
trumpet

农历　nónglì
Chinese lunar calender

壮观　zhuàngguān
spectacular

温和　wēnhé
mild

宜人　yírén
pleasant

舒适　shūshì
comfortable

向往　xiàngwǎng
to yearn for

幸福感　xìngfúgǎn
sense of happiness

仅次于　jǐn cì yú
second only to...

成千上万

chéngqiān shàngwàn
thousands of

为西湖增添了许多历史气息。

古老的京杭大运河的终点在杭州，现在也已经成了旅游景点之一。坐在船上，可以欣赏运河两岸的美景。

杭州的钱塘江大潮也非常有名。钱塘江入海口是个喇叭口，受月球引力的影响，每年农历八月中旬就会形成非常壮观的钱塘江大潮，吸引了众多游客前去观看。

苏州和杭州的气候也非常温和，特别是春天和秋天，十分宜人。

杭州的生活非常舒适，令人向往。根据2011年的一个调查，杭州人民的幸福感非常高，在全国排第二名，仅次于成都市。

苏州和杭州都是闻名中外的旅游城市，每天都有成千上万来自全国各地和世界各国的游客到这里旅游，欣赏美景，享受美食。看到这里，你是不是也想到人间天堂苏州和杭州去看看呢？

京杭大运河杭州段

124

Hangzhou is the end of Beijing-Hangzhou Canal, which is now also one of the tourist destinations. One can enjoy the beautiful scenery of the canal banks when he sits in a boat.

钱塘江大潮

Qiantang Tide of Hangzhou is also very famous, the mouth of which is like a trumpet. Under the influence of lunar attraction, the magnificent Qiantang Tide is formed in each mid-August in Chinese lunar calendar, which attracts numerous tourists to the scene.

The weather is very mild and pleasant in Suzhou and Hangzhou, especially in spring and autumn.

People in Hangzhou enjoy a comfortable life, and many people elsewhere yearn for living there. A survey of 2011 showed that people of Hangzhou had a very high sense of happiness, ranking only second to people of Chengdu City.

Both Suzhou and Hangzhou are tourist destinations famous in China and around the world. Thousands of tourists from home and abroad come here to enjoy the beautiful scenery and delicious food. Would you like to go to Suzhou and Hangzhou and have a look at the paradise on earth, too?

文化注释

❶ 白蛇传

　　白素贞是千年修炼的白蛇，为了报答许仙前世的救命之恩，变成人来到人间，后来遇到青蛇小青，两人结伴。白素贞施展法力，与许仙相识，并嫁给了他。后来法海说服许仙在端午节让白素贞喝下带有雄黄的酒，白素贞不得不现出蛇的原形，吓死了许仙。白素贞上天庭盗取仙草将许仙救活。法海将许仙骗到金山寺并把他软禁起来，白素贞、小青一起与法海斗法，水漫金山寺，却因此伤害了其他生灵。白素贞触犯天法，在生下孩子后被法海收入钵内，镇压在雷峰塔下。后来白素贞的儿子长大后考试中了状元，他来到雷峰塔前，与小青一起将白素贞救出，全家团聚。

◇ 练习 ◇

▬ 阅读理解 Reading comprehension

练习1：判断正误 Decide whether the following statements are right (√) or wrong (×)

例 "苏杭"是指中国的苏州和杭州两个地方。(√)

1. 明清时期，苏州是中国最繁华的地区之一。(　)

2. 苏州园林的特点就是在每一个点上都放了一幅完美的画儿。(　)

3. 留园建于明代，是苏州最有名的园林之一。(　)

4. 北京的颐和园比苏州的拙政园规模要小得多。(　)

5. 刺绣是苏州非常有名的手工艺品。(　)

6. 西湖在杭州市内，三面环水。(　)

7. 夏天，西湖是观赏荷花的好地方。（　　）

8. 每年农历八月中旬都会有非常壮观的钱塘江大潮。（　　）

9. 雷峰塔、岳飞庙是苏州两个著名的旅游景点。（　　）

10. 苏州和杭州的气候非常温和，春天和秋天的天气，不冷也不热。（　　）

练习2：选择正确答案 Choose the right answers

例 明清时期，苏州是中国最 ___B___ 的地区之一。

　A. 古老　　　　　B. 繁华　　　　　C. 有名　　　　　D. 有特色

1. 苏州园林的特点就是：游客 _____ 站在哪个点上，眼前总是一幅图画。

　A. 无论　　　　　B. 即使　　　　　C. 不但　　　　　D. 而且

2. _____ 去过苏州的人，没有一个不称赞苏州那些各具特色的园林。

　A. 确实　　　　　B. 除了　　　　　C. 凡是　　　　　D. 只有

3. 明清时期，苏州有许多 _____ 、各具特色的私家园林。

　A. 前前后后　　B. 大大小小　　C. 高高低低　　D. 远远近近

4. _____ 是亭台楼阁、假山池塘，_____ 是游廊门窗、花草树木，
_____ 让游览者产生"如在图画中"的感觉。

　A. 不但……而且……都……　　　　B. 无论……还……都……

　C. 不仅……还……都……　　　　　D. 不管……都……还……

5. 与承德的避暑山庄相比，拙政园的规模 _____ 。

　A. 小得多　　　　B. 大得多　　　　C. 美得多　　　　D. 有名得多

6. _____ 是中国的"四大名园"之一。

　A. 西湖　　　　　B. 灵隐寺　　　　C. 颐和园　　　　D. 虎跑泉

7. 马可·波罗称杭州为世界上 _____ 之城。

   A. 物产最丰富   B. 气候宜人   C. 最美丽华贵   D. 工艺品最有名

8. 西湖附近的岳飞庙，为西湖增添了许多 _____ 。

   A. 赏荷花的地方   B. 美丽的景色   C. 幸福感   D. 历史气息

9. 钱塘江入海口是喇叭口，由于 _____ 的影响，每年都会形成非常壮观的钱塘江大潮。

   A. 受月球引力的影响   B. 杭州的气候

   C. 三面环山   D. 八月中旬

10. 杭州西湖春天的美景是 _____ 。

   A. 雪后的美景   B. 湖中的荷花   C. 明亮的月亮   D. 湖边的绿柳红花

语段练习 Exercises about paragraphs

连线 **Match the statements on the left with those on the right**

1. 苏州位于江苏省的南部   A. 没有不被杭州西湖的风景所吸引

2. 苏州的各个园林各具特色   B. 苏州最有名的园林之一

3. 明清时期，苏州有许多私家花园   C. 古代的美女西施

4. 凡是去过杭州的人   D. 至今已有 2500 多年的历史

5. "上有天堂，下有苏杭"意思是说   E. 但是它们都有一个共同的特点

6. 拙政园是   F. "世界上最美丽华贵之城"

7. 杭州的历史很长，曾经是   G. 大大小小 500 多个

8. 人们常常把西湖比作   H. 苏州和杭州非常美，就像天堂一样

9. 杭州最有名的景点是   I. 南宋时期的首都

10. 杭州被马可·波罗称为   J. 三面环山的西湖

三 词汇练习 Exercises about vocabulary

用本课所学的新词填空 Fill in the blanks with the new words in this lesson

典型	无论	繁华	宜人	完美
不管	四季	壮观	景点	保存

中国有一句话，"上有天堂，下有苏杭"，意思是说，苏州和杭州非常美，就像天堂一样。苏州位于江苏省的南部，明清时期，是中国最 <u>繁华</u> 的地区之一。苏州最有名的是苏州园林，其特点就是游客 _____ 站在哪个点上，眼前总是一幅 _____ 的图画。现在 _____ 完好的有十几处，其中最有名的园林是建于明代的拙政园和建于清代的留园，它们是中国南方地区民间建筑的 _____ 代表，与北京的颐和园、承德的避暑山庄一起被称为中国的"四大名园"。杭州最有名的 _____ 是西湖。西湖一年四季都有不同的美景，有人说西湖好像一个美女，_____ 怎么打扮，都非常漂亮。西湖一年 _____ 都很美：春天的绿柳红花，夏天湖中的荷花，秋天晚上的月亮，冬天西湖的白雪。杭州的钱塘江大潮也非常 _____ 。总之苏州、杭州的气候非常 _____ ，是中国非常有名的旅游城市。

四 语法练习 Exercises about grammar

用所给的词语组句 Make sentences with the words given

例 地区 苏州 是 最繁华的 明清时期 中国 之一

<u>明清时期，苏州是中国最繁华的地区之一。</u>

1. 苏州 上海 离 近 很 最大的 中国 城市

_____

2. 典型代表　民间建筑的　是　中国　南方地区　它们

_____

3. 西湖　西施　把　比作　有人　美女　古代的

_____

4. 钱塘江大潮　就会　农历　形成　八月中旬　非常壮观的　每年

_____

5. 苏州和杭州的　非常温和　也　春天　特别是　和秋天　气候　十分宜人

_____

五 写作练习 Writing practice

用下列词语造句 **Make sentences using the following words and phrases**

1. 凡是……没有一个不……：_____

2. 被……所吸引：_____

3. 各具特色：_____

4. 最……之一：_____

5. 大大小小：_____

6. 无论……都：_____

7. 特别是：_____

8. 不管……都：_____

9. 令人向往：_____

10. 仅次于：_____

桂林山水甲天下 10

桂林山水像是一幅秀丽的山水画

导读问题　Lead-in questions

1. 上图中的山水非常有特色，你去过类似的地方吗？
2. "桂林山水甲天下"是什么意思？
3. 桂林都有哪些山和河流？它们的名字都是怎么得来的？
4. 桂林的溶洞是怎么形成的？
5. 如果你是导游，你打算怎么向你的游客介绍桂林呢？

甲　jiǎ
No.1, the best

天下　tiānxià
under heaven

独一无二　dúyī wú'èr
unique

广西壮族自治区
Guǎngxī Zhuàngzú Zìzhìqū
Guangxi Zhuang Autonomous Region

胜地　shèngdì
resort

之所以　zhīsuǒyǐ
the reason why...

桂花　guìhuā
laurel flower

盛开　shèngkāi
to bloom

青　qīng
green

秀　xiù
beautiful

洞　dòng
cave

象鼻山　Xiàngbí Shān
Elephant's Trunk Hill

标志性　biāozhìxìng
landmark

漓江　Lí Jiāng
Li River

"桂林山水甲天下"，大家都知道这句话。"甲"在这里是"第一"的意思，意思是说桂林的山水美景是天下独一无二的。

广西桂林风光

桂林是中国南方的一个美丽城市，位于广西壮族自治区的东北部，是中国十大旅游胜地①之一。桂林之所以叫桂林，是因为那里有很多桂树林。想象一下，桂花处处盛开的桂林该是多么美丽啊！

桂林的山水有四美：山青、水秀、洞奇、石美。

桂林的山，各不相连，平地拔起，千姿百态，非常奇特。这里的山，四季常青，有着很有趣的名字。其中最有名的是象鼻山，它的形状特别像一只大象站在漓江边用鼻子喝水，被认为是桂林山水的标志性景点之一。

漓江全长160公里，是世界上最

Every Chinese knows the sentence, "桂林山水甲天下", meaning "Guilin has the best landscape under heaven". "甲" here means "No. 1" or "the best".

Situated in northeast Guangxi Zhuang Autonomous Region and being one of China's top ten tourist resorts, Guilin is a beautiful city of south China. It is said that the city of Guilin got its name because it is covered with dense laurel forests. Just imagine. How beautiful Guilin would be if every part of it blooms with laurel flowers!

远处的山像一个骆驼在过江

The beauty of Guilin lies in its green mountains, beautiful water, bizarre caves and gorgeous rocks.

Being disconnected and protruding, the mountains in Guilin are oddly shaped. Each of these evergreen mountains has an interesting name. Regarded as one of the landmark landscapes of Guilin, Elephant Trunk Hill is the most famous hill, resembling an elephant drinking the water of Li River using its nose.

As is said, "Guilin has the best landscape under heaven"; in fact, the landscape of Li River is the best of Guilin. Being one of the most beautiful rivers

象鼻山，像一个大象在吸水

133

清澈　qīngchè
clear

透明　tòumíng
transparent

倒影　dàoyǐng
inverted reflection in the water

奇观　qíguān
wonder

山峰　shānfēng
peak

缓缓　huǎnhuǎn
slowly

秀丽　xiùlì
beautiful

喀斯特地貌　kāsītè dìmào
karst landform

溶洞　róngdòng
limestone cave

垂　chuí
to hang

形态各异　xíngtài gè yì
diverse in form

凤　fèng
phoenix

蛇　shé
snake

形态　xíngtài
form

大自然　dàzìrán
Mother Nature

人工　réngōng
man-made

秀丽的河流之一。都说"桂林山水甲天下"，其实还有一句"漓江山水甲桂林"呢！桂林最美的就是漓江。漓江的"漓"字，是清澈、透明的意思，漓江的江水十分清澈，甚至可以清楚地看到江底的石头。倒影是漓江的一大奇观，当你坐着小船，从水中山峰的倒影上缓缓经过时，你会发现，漓江的每个地方，都是一幅秀丽的中国山水画，真是一种享受！

乘船欣赏如画的漓江山水

桂林山水属于典型的喀斯特地貌，有许多有趣的溶洞。洞中有很多从洞顶上垂下来的奇石，形态各异，有的像龙，有的像凤，有的像蛇，还有的像花，非常特别。这些形态各异的石头，全都是大自然经过上千年、上万年的时间，一点一点雕琢形成的，没有一点人工

in the world with a total length of 160 kilometers, Li River is the most beautiful scenic spot in Guilin. "Li" means crystal clear. The water of Li River is so limpid that one can even clearly see the stones at the bottom of the river. Inverted reflections in the water are one of the wonders of Li River. When you are sitting

漓江中的倒影清晰可见

in a small boat slowly passing the inverted reflections of mountains in the water, you'll find every part of Li River is like a beautiful Chinese painting. You'll really enjoy it!

The landscape of Guilin belongs to the typical karst landform, where many interesting limestone caves can be found. There are many strange stones hanging from the top of these caves. Being diverse in form, some resemble dragons, some are in the shape of phoenixes, some are like snakes, while others look like flowers. All these odd stones are not man-made, but are gradually shaped by Mother Nature over thousands of years, which make people marvel at the magic power of nature.

Besides the green mountains, beautiful water, bizarre caves and gorgeous rocks, Guilin is also

喀斯特地貌形成的溶洞奇观

痕迹 hénjì
trace

神奇 shénqí
magic

龙胜山 Lóngshèng Shān
Longsheng Mountain

梯田 tītián
terrace

元朝 Yuáncháo
Yuan Dynasty

修建 xiūjiàn
to construct, to build

清朝 Qīngcháo
Qing Dynasty

季节 jìjié
season

银色 yínsè
(of colour) silver

围绕 wéirào
to surround

禾苗 hémiáo
cereal seedlings

结（果实） jié (guǒshí)
to bear (fruits)

果实 guǒshí
fruit

宝塔 bǎotǎ
pagoda

项链 xiàngliàn
necklace

好客 hàokè
hospitable

欣赏 xīnshǎng
to enjoy

流连忘返 liúlián wàngfǎn
to linger on

痕迹，让人感叹大自然的神奇魔力！

　　除了"四美"以外，桂林龙胜山上的龙胜梯田也非常有名。龙胜梯田从元朝就开始修建，一直到清朝才建好。不同的季节，龙胜梯田有着不同的美丽风景。春天，田里都是水，远远地看着龙胜梯田，就好像是一条条银色的带子围绕在山上；夏天，田里的禾苗长大了，一层一层的梯田就像给大山穿上了绿色的衣服；秋天，禾苗结出金黄的果实，大山就变成了金色的宝塔；冬天，一场大雪，梯田上便盖了一层厚厚的白雪，远远望去，大山就像戴上了白玉做的项链。无论什么时候，龙胜梯田都能带给你美的享受。

春天的龙胜梯田

　　看到这里，你是不是也很想到桂林去旅游呢？桂林的人们友好、热情、好客，欢迎你来桂林，欣赏这里迷人的风景，相信你一定会流连忘返！

famous for Longsheng Terrace on Longsheng Mountain. Built from the Yuan Dynasty to the Qing Dynasty, Longsheng Terrace has different beautiful sceneries in different seasons. In spring, the fields are filled with water. Viewing Longsheng Terrace from afar, they look like silver belts surrounding the mountain. In summer, after the seedlings in the fields grow

秋天的龙胜梯田

up, the mountain seems to be dressed in green clothes. In autumn, after the seedlings bear golden fruits, the mountain becomes a golden pagoda. In winter, after the terrace is covered with snow, looking from afar, the

mountain seems to be wearing white jade necklaces. Whenever you go there, you'll fully enjoy the beauty of Longsheng Terrace.

At this point, are you thinking of traveling to Guilin, too? The people in Guilin are friendly and hospitable, and the scenery there is fascinating. Welcome to Guilin! You'll surely enjoy it!

桂林阳朔农村风光

137

文化注释

❶ 中国十大旅游胜地

中国十大旅游胜地分别是：万里长城、北京故宫、承德避暑山庄、安徽黄山、杭州西湖、桂林山水、西安兵马俑、苏州园林、长江三峡、台湾日月潭。

◇ 练习 ◇

一 阅读理解 Reading comprehension

练习1：判断正误 Decide whether the following statements are right（√）or wrong（×）

例 桂林位于中国广西壮族自治区的西北部。（ × ）

1. 在中国，大家都知道"桂林山水甲天下"这句话。（ ）

2. "甲"是"第一"的意思。（ ）

3. 桂林是中国南方的一个美丽城市，是中国著名的旅游胜地。（ ）

4. 桂林有很多桂树林、桂花，因而得名。（ ）

5. 象鼻山是桂林山水的标志性景点之一。（ ）

6. 桂林的山水有四美：山青、水秀、洞奇、梯田美。

7. 漓江全长160公里，是世界上最秀丽的河流之一。（ ）

8. 桂林溶洞的石头全都是手工一点一点做成的。（ ）

9. 龙胜梯田全都是大自然形成的，没有一点人类手工的痕迹。（ ）

10. 一年四季中，龙胜梯田只有春天很美。（ ）

练习 2：选择正确答案 **Choose the right answers**

例 桂林位于中国广西壮族自治区的东北部，是中国十大 _____B_____ 之一。

　　A. 美丽城市　　　　B. 旅游胜地　　　　C. 最有名的山　　　D. 奇观

1. 桂林之所以叫桂林，是因为那里有 _____ 。

　　A. 溶洞　　　　　　B. 象鼻山　　　　　C. 漓江　　　　　　D. 很多桂树林

2. 桂林是一个位于中国 _____ 的美丽城市。

　　A. 东北　　　　　　B. 北方　　　　　　C. 东方　　　　　　D. 南方

3. 桂林风景有四大特点：山青、水秀、_____ 、石美。

　　A. 洞奇　　　　　　B. 梯田　　　　　　C. 灌木　　　　　　D. 宝塔

4. 象鼻山被认为是桂林山水的 _____ 景点之一。

　　A. 清澈　　　　　　B. 关键性　　　　　C. 标志性　　　　　D. 特别

5. "漓江山水甲桂林"意思是说 _____ 。

　　A. 漓江的山水在桂林是最美丽的

　　B. 桂林被称为漓江山水

　　C. 桂林离漓江山水不远

　　D. 漓江山水的形状很美

6. 当你坐着小船经过水中山峰倒影时，你会发现漓江的每一个地方，都是
　　_____ 秀丽的中国山水画。

　　A. 一个　　　　　　B. 一张　　　　　　C. 一幅　　　　　　D. 一副

7. 桂林的 _____ 包括许多有趣的溶洞。

　　A. 独一无二　　　　　　　　　　　B. 喀斯特地貌

　　C. 形态各异　　　　　　　　　　　D. 雕琢

8. _____ 是漓江的一大奇观。

    A. 宝塔　　　　　B. 钓鱼　　　　　C. 禾苗　　　　　D. 倒影

9. 冬天，龙胜梯田里有厚厚的白雪，大山就像戴上了白玉做的 _____ 。

    A. 果实　　　　　B. 桂花　　　　　C. 项链　　　　　D. 倒影

10. _____ 什么时候，龙胜梯田都能带给你美的享受。

    A. 尽管　　　　　B. 而且　　　　　C. 不论　　　　　D. 不仅

语段练习 Exercises about paragraphs

连线 Match the statements on the left with those on the right

1. 桂林是一个美丽的城市　　　　　　A. 一只大象站在漓江边在用鼻子喝水

2. 象鼻山的形状特别像　　　　　　　B. 最秀丽的河流之一

3. 龙胜梯田从元朝就开始修建　　　　C. 甚至可以清楚地看见江底的石头

4. 在不同的季节，龙胜梯田有着　　　D. 是中国十大旅游胜地之一

5. 桂林的漓江是世界上　　　　　　　E. 清澈、透明的意思

6. 漓江的"漓"字是　　　　　　　　F. 许多有趣的溶洞

7. 春天龙胜一层层的梯田就好像　　　G. 秀丽的中国山水画

8. 漓江的水非常清澈　　　　　　　　H. 不同的美丽风景

9. 漓江的每个地方，都是一幅　　　　I. 一直到清朝才建好

10. 桂林奇特的喀斯特地貌包括　　　　J. 一条条银色的带子围绕在山上

三 词汇练习 Exercises about vocabulary

用本课所学的新词填空 Fill in the blanks with the new words in this lesson

倒影	享受	痕迹	形态	旅游胜地
形状	季节	无论	清澈	独一无二

　　桂林是中国十大旅游胜地之一。人人都知道"桂林山水甲天下"，意思是说桂林的风景是天下 <u>独一无二</u> 的。桂林最有名的山是漓江右岸的象鼻山。象鼻山因为 _____ 特别像是一只大象站在漓江边用鼻子喝水，所以被人们叫作象鼻山。桂林最美的是漓江，它是世界上最秀丽的河流之一。漓江的江水十分 _____ 、透明。坐着小船，从水中山峰的 _____ 上缓缓经过，是一种美好的 _____ 。桂林的溶洞，非常有特色，这些溶洞属于奇特的喀斯特地貌，溶洞中有许多从洞顶上垂下来的石头，_____ 各异。这些不同的形状全都是大自然一点一点形成的，没有一点人工的 _____ 。龙胜山上的龙胜梯田也很有名，不同的 _____ ，龙胜梯田有着不同的美丽风景。_____ 哪个季节去龙胜梯田游玩都是一个好选择。

四 语法练习 Exercises about grammar

用所给的词语组句 Make sentences with the words given

例　桂林　是因为　之所以　那里　叫桂林　很多　有　桂树林

　　<u>桂林之所以叫桂林，是因为那里有很多桂树林。</u>

1. 喝水　形状　它的　一只　特别　漓江边　站在　像　用鼻子　大象

_____

2. 漓江的　地方　都是　每一个　秀丽的　中国山水画　一幅

---

3. 桂林的山水　典型　喀斯特　属于　地貌

---

4. 很多　洞中　有　洞顶　从　上　下来　垂　的　奇石

---

5. 无论　时候　什么　龙胜　都能　梯田　带给　美的享受　你

五 写作练习 Writing practice

用下列词语造句 Make sentences using the following words and phrases

1. 独一无二：_____

2. 之所以……是因为：_____

3. 多么……啊：_____

4. 千姿百态：_____

5. 标志性：_____

6. 有的……有的……还有的……：_____

7. 一直到……才……：_____

8. 就好像……：_____

9. 无论……都……：_____

10. 流连忘返：_____

生词表 Vocabulary

生词	拼音	课号
A		
阿訇	āhōng	3
挨	āi	8
B		
搬迁	bānqiān	8
板块	bǎnkuài	7
半路	bànlù	7
包括	bāokuò	2,7
包容	bāoróng	5
宝塔	bǎotǎ	10
北半球	běibànqiú	4
北极	běijí	7
北纬	běiwěi	8
本底	běndǐ	7
比喻	bǐyù	6
边界	biānjiè	1
边缘	biānyuán	2
鞭	biān	8
标志性	biāozhìxìng	10
濒危	bīnwēi	7
冰川	bīngchuān	7
冰封	bīng fēng	4
C		
草原	cǎoyuán	8
侧面	cèmiàn	6

差别	chābié	4
差异	chāyì	4
茶饭不思	cháfàn bùsī	8
长眠	chángmián	7
朝代	cháodài	5
朝代	cháodài	6
称赞	chēngzàn	9
成千上万	chéngqiān shàngwàn	10
成群	chéngqún	8
城际	chéngjì	1
城镇	chéngzhèn	3
乘	chéng	1
池塘	chítáng	9
赤道	chìdào	3
传遍	chuánbiàn	8
传出	chuánchū	8
传说	chuánshuō	5,6
垂	chuí	10
刺绣	cìxiù	9
D		
大旱	dà hàn	6
大陆	dàlù	1
大自然	dàzìrán	10
戴	dài	3
单程	dānchéng	1

挡住	dǎngzhù	7	飞翔	fēixiáng	8
岛屿	dǎoyǔ	1	肥沃	féiwò	2
倒影	dàoyǐng	10	分布	fēnbù	1,3,7
低度	dīdù	4	芬芳	fēnfāng	5
地理	dìlǐ	4	风景	fēngjǐng	9
地貌	dìmào	7	凤	fèng	10
地势	dìshì	2	夫妇	fūfù	3
地毯	dìtǎn	8	副业	fùyè	2
地位	dìwèi	1	覆盖	fùgài	2,7
地形	dìxíng	2		**G**	
地质	dìzhì	7	干燥	gānzào	7
典型	diǎnxíng	9	港口	gǎngkǒu	1
点缀	diǎnzhuì	8	高低起伏	gāo dī qǐfú	2
雕	diāo	4	高峰	gāo fēng	5
雕刻	diāokè	8	高铁	gāotiě	1
冬季	dōngjì	4	高原	gāoyuán	2
动脉	dòngmài	6	高原反应	gāoyuán fǎnyìng	4
动人	dòngrén	8	格外	géwài	5
洞	dòng	10	耕地	gēngdì	2.4
独特	dútè	7	公元前	gōngyuán qián	9
独一无二	dúyī wú'èr	10	贡献	gòngxiàn	3
度假	dùjià	4	沟通	gōutōng	2
多种多样	duōzhǒng duōyàng	2	观赏	guānshǎng	4
	F		冠军	guànjūn	8
凡是	fánshì	9	贯穿	guànchuān	6
繁华	fánhuá	9	广阔	guǎngkuò	2
防晒	fángshài	7	规模	guīmó	9

桂花	guìhuā	10
国土	guótǔ	4
果实	guǒshí	10

	H	
海拔	hǎibá	2,5,7
海洋	hǎiyáng	1,4
含蓄	hánxù	4
寒冷	hánlěng	4
旱	hàn	4
好客	hàokè	8,10
禾苗	hémiáo	10
和睦	hémù	5
和谐	héxié	1,5
河段	héduàn	6
荷花	héhuā	9
痕迹	hénjì	10
横卧	héng wò	6
华贵	huáguì	9
滑冰	huá bīng	4
滑雪	huá xuě	4
欢快	huānkuài	8
环	huán	9
缓缓	huǎnhuǎn	10
缓慢	huǎnmàn	4
皇帝	huángdì	5
皇家	huángjiā	9
挥	huī	8

汇成	huìchéng	3
火炉	huǒlú	4
货运量	huòyùnliàng	6

	J	
几乎	jīhū	4
计划生育	jìhuà shēngyù	3
季风	jìfēng	4
季节	jìjié	10
祭拜	jìbài	5
甲	jiǎ	10
假山	jiǎshān	9
减缓	jiǎnhuǎn	4
建筑	jiànzhù	5,9
箭	jiàn	8
降水	jiàngshuǐ	4
阶梯	jiētī	2
节奏	jiézòu	4
结（果实）	jié (guǒshí)	10
截止	jiézhǐ	3
筋骨	jīngǔ	8
仅次于	jǐn cì yú	9
惊喜	jīngxǐ	4
景点	jǐngdiǎn	9
竟然	jìngrán	7
举足轻重	jǔzú qīngzhòng	1
巨人	jùrén	5
剧烈	jùliè	7

暖湿	nuǎnshī	7

P

排名	pái míng	1
派	pài	5
袍	páo	8
盆地	péndì	2
澎湃	péngpài	6
皮袄	pí'ǎo	4
飘	piāo	4,8
飘逸	piāoyì	8
平坦	píngtǎn	2
平原	píngyuán	2,5
普遍	pǔbiàn	4
瀑布	pùbù	6

Q

奇观	qíguān	10
奇异	qīyì	2
崎岖	qíqū	2
起初	qǐchū	7
气候	qìhòu	4
气息	qìxī	9
侵蚀	qīnshí	2
青	qīng	10
清澈	qīngchè	10
清香	qīngxiāng	8
清新	qīngxīn	8
丘陵	qiūlíng	2

区域	qūyù	1
趋势	qūshì	2
圈	quān	3
全长	quáncháng	6

R

热量	rèliàng	4
热门	rèmén	5
热闹	rènao	8
人工	réngōng	10
人间	rénjiān	6
人文	rénwén	4
溶洞	róngdòng	10
溶解	róngjiě	2
融水	róngshuǐ	7

S

赛	sài	8
散布	sànbù	8
纱	shā	4
山峰	shānfēng	10
扇	shàn	9
擅长	shàncháng	8
上游	shàngyóu	1
少数民族	shǎoshù mínzú	3
蛇	shé	10
射	shè	8
神话	shénhuà	5,7
神奇	shénqí	10

吸引	xīyǐn	6,9
稀薄	xībó	4,7
夏季	xiàjì	4
鲜花	xiānhuā	4
险	xiǎn	5
相对	xiāngduì	4
相连	xiānglián	1
相宜	xiāngyí	9
享受	xiǎngshòu	4
享有	xiǎngyǒu	6
向往	xiàngwǎng	7,9
项链	xiàngliàn	10
潇洒	xiāosǎ	8
小吃	xiǎochī	9
小伙子	xiǎohuǒzi	8
小麦	xiǎomài	4
写照	xiězhào	4
欣赏	xīnshǎng	10
信仰	xìnyǎng	3
行使	xíngshǐ	2
形成	xíngchéng	7
形态	xíngtài	2,10
形态各异	xíngtài gè yì	10
形影不离	xíngyǐng bùlí	8
醒来	xǐnglái	8
幸福感	xìngfúgǎn	9

汹涌	xiōngyǒng	6
雄浑	xiónghún	5
雄伟	xióngwěi	5
雄姿	xióngzī	5
修建	xiūjiàn	10
秀	xiù	10
秀丽	xiùlì	5,10
畜牧业	xùmùyè	2
选择	xuǎnzé	4
靴	xuē	8
寻找	xúnzhǎo	5

Y

延续	yánxù	5
沿岸	yán'àn	6
沿海	yánhǎi	1
养成	yǎngchéng	4
氧气	yǎngqì	4,7
遥远	yáoyuǎn	6
夜晚	yèwǎn	4
一览众山小	yì lǎn zhòng shān xiǎo	5
一望无际	yíwàng wújì	2,8
一系列	yíxìliè	2
宜人	yírén	9
亿	yì	7
因而	yīn'ér	5
因素	yīnsù	1

银色	yínsè	10
英尺	yīngchǐ	5
婴儿	yīng'ér	3
悠久	yōujiǔ	6
悠扬	yōuyáng	8
游客	yóukè	9
游廊	yóuláng	9
游牧	yóumù	8
园林	yuánlín	9
原始	yuánshǐ	6
岳	yuè	5
运河	yùnhé	9
蕴藏	yùncáng	2

Z		
赞美	zànměi	5
增添	zēngtiān	9
展示	zhǎnshì	5
战场	zhànchǎng	6
战胜	zhànshèng	6
湛蓝	zhànlán	8
招待	zhāodài	8

珍稀	zhēnxī	7
拯救	zhěngjiù	6
政策	zhèngcè	3
之所以	zhīsuǒyǐ	10
直辖市	zhíxiáshì	1
植物	zhíwù	4
中轴线	zhōngzhóuxiàn	5
重心	zhòngxīn	6
昼夜	zhòuyè	4
逐渐	zhújiàn	4,6
主食	zhǔshí	4
著名	zhùmíng	5
转移	zhuǎnyí	6
壮	zhuàng	6
壮观	zhuàngguān	6,9
壮美	zhuàngměi	5
自治区	zìzhìqū	6
足迹	zújì	6
组成	zǔchéng	1
坐落	zuòluò	1,5

专有名词 Proper Nouns

生词	拼音	课号
A		
安徽	Ānhuī	6
B		
白帝城	Báidìchéng	6
《白蛇传》	Báishé Zhuàn	9
避暑山庄	Bìshǔ Shānzhuāng	9
C		
承德	Chéngdé	9
D		
傣族	Dǎizú	3
道教	Dàojiào	5
F		
方丈	Fāngzhàng	5
汾渭平原	Fén Wèi Píngyuán	2
佛教	Fójiào	5
G		
广西壮族自治区	Guǎngxī Zhuàngzú Zìzhìqū	10
H		
恒山	Héng Shān	5
衡山	Héng Shān	5
壶口	Húkǒu	6
火把节	Huǒbǎ Jié	3

生词	拼音	课号
L		
雷峰塔	Léifēng Tǎ	9
漓江	Lí Jiāng	10
李白	Lǐ Bái	6
龙胜山	Lóngshèng Shān	10
芦笙节	Lúshēng Jié	3
M		
马可·波罗	Mǎkě · Bōluó	9
蒙古族	Ménggǔzú	3
漠河	Mòhé	4
N		
内蒙古	Nèiměnggǔ	8
尼泊尔	Níbó'ěr	7
P		
蓬莱	Pénglái	5
泼水节	Pōshuǐ Jié	3
Q		
钱塘江大潮	Qiántáng Jiāng Dàcháo	9
青藏高原	Qīng–Zàng Gāoyuán	6,7
清朝	Qīngcháo	10
R		
儒家	Rújiā	5